27 ✓

THE YALE SHAKESPEARE

EDITED BY

WILBUR L. CROSS   TUCKER BROOKE

WILLARD HIGLEY DURHAM

PUBLISHED UNDER THE DIRECTION

OF THE

DEPARTMENT OF ENGLISH, YALE UNIVERSITY,

ON THE FUND

GIVEN TO THE YALE UNIVERSITY PRESS IN 1917

BY THE MEMBERS OF THE

KINGSLEY TRUST ASSOCIATION

TO COMMEMORATE THE SEVENTY-FIFTH ANNIVERSARY

OF THE FOUNDING OF THE SOCIETY

·: *The Yale Shakespeare* :·

A MIDSUMMER NIGHT'S DREAM

EDITED BY

WILLARD HIGLEY DURHAM

NEW HAVEN · YALE UNIVERSITY PRESS
LONDON · OXFORD UNIVERSITY PRESS

TABLE OF CONTENTS

		PAGE
THE TEXT	. . . . . .	1
NOTES	. . . . . .	80
APPENDIX A.	Sources of the Play . .	88
APPENDIX B.	The History of the Play .	89
APPENDIX C.	The Text of the Present Edition	91
APPENDIX D.	Suggestions for Collateral Reading . . .	92
INDEX OF WORDS GLOSSED		93

The facsimile opposite represents the unusually handsome title-page of the genuine edition of 1600. The photograph is made from the Elizabethan Club copy, which was formerly in the Heber, Daniel, and Huth libraries. Seven other copies of this edition are known.

A Midſommer nights dreame.

As it hath beene ſundry times pub-
lickely acted, by the *Right honoura-*
ble, the Lord Chamberlaine his
ſeruants.

Written by William Shakeſpeare.

¶ Imprinted at London, for *Thomas Fiſher*, and are to
be ſoulde at his ſhoppe, at the Signe of the White Hart,
in *Fleetſtreete*, 1600.

[DRAMATIS PERSONÆ

THESEUS, *Duke of Athens*

EGEUS, *Father to Hermia*

LYSANDER,
DEMETRIUS, } *in love with Hermia*

PHILOSTRATE, *Master of the Revels to Theseus*

QUINCE, *a Carpenter*

SNUG, *a Joiner*

BOTTOM, *a Weaver*

FLUTE, *a Bellows-mender*

SNOUT, *a Tinker*

STARVELING, *a Tailor*

HIPPOLYTA, *Queen of the Amazons, betrothed to Theseus*

HERMIA, *Daughter to Egeus, in love with Lysander*

HELENA, *in love with Demetrius*

OBERON, *King of the Fairies*

TITANIA, *Queen of the Fairies*

PUCK, *or Robin Goodfellow*

PEASE-BLOSSOM,
COBWEB,
MOTH, } *Fairies*
MUSTARD-SEED,

Other Fairies attending their King and Queen
Attendants on Theseus and Hippolyta

SCENE: *Athens, and a Wood near it.*]

A Midsummer Night's Dream

ACT FIRST

Scene One

[*Athens. The Palace of Theseus*]

Enter Theseus, Hippolyta, with [*Philostrate and*]
others.

The. Now, fair Hippolyta, our nuptial hour   *ANTICIPATION*
Draws on apace: four happy days bring in   *OF MARRIAGE*
Another moon; but O! methinks how slow   *+ ENTERTAIN-*
This old moon wanes; she lingers my desires,   4   *MENT*
Like to a step-dame, or a dowager
Long withering out a young man's revenue.
  Hip. Four days will quickly steep themselves in
    night;
Four nights will quickly dream away the time;   8
And then the moon, like to a silver bow
New-bent in heaven, shall behold the night
Of our solemnities.
    The.   Go, Philostrate,
Stir up the Athenian youth to merriments;   12
Awake the pert and nimble spirit of mirth;
Turn melancholy forth to funerals;
The pale companion is not for our pomp.
                    [*Exit Philostrate.*]
Hippolyta, I woo'd thee with my sword,   16
And won thy love doing thee injuries;
But I will wed thee in another key,
With pomp, with triumph, and with revelling.

4 lingers: *delays fulfillment of*   5, 6 *Cf. n.*   13 pert: *lively*
15 pomp: *ceremonial procession*   19 triumph: *festive entertainment*

Enter Egeus and his daughter Hermia, Lysander,
and Demetrius.

Ege. Happy be Theseus, our renowned duke!

The. Thanks, good Egeus: what's the news with
thee?

Ege. Full of vexation come I, with complaint
Against my child, my daughter Hermia.
Stand forth, Demetrius. My noble lord,   24
This man hath my consent to marry her.
Stand forth, Lysander: and, my gracious duke,
This man hath bewitch'd the bosom of my child:
Thou, thou, Lysander, thou hast given her rimes,
And interchang'd love-tokens with my child;   29
Thou hast by moonlight at her window sung,
With feigning voice, verses of feigning love;
And stol'n the impression of her fantasy   32
With bracelets of thy hair, rings, gawds, conceits,
Knacks, trifles, nosegays, sweetmeats, messengers
Of strong prevailment in unharden'd youth;
With cunning hast thou filch'd my daughter's
heart;   36
Turn'd her obedience, which is due to me,
To stubborn harshness. And, my gracious duke,
Be it so she will not here before your Grace
Consent to marry with Demetrius,   40
I beg the ancient privilege of Athens,
As she is mine, I may dispose of her;
Which shall be either to this gentleman,
Or to her death, according to our law   44
Immediately provided in that case.

The. What say you, Hermia? be advis'd, fair maid.
To you your father should be as a god;

---

31 feigning; *cf. n.*   32 fantasy: *imagination; cf. n.*
33 gawds: *gewgaws*   conceits: *fancy articles*
34 Knacks: *knickknacks*   45 Immediately: *expressly*

One that compos'd your beauties, yea, and one
To whom you are but as a <u>form</u> in wax   49
<u>By him imprinted</u>, and within his power   NATURE +
To leave the figure or disfigure it.   CHARACTER
Demetrius is a worthy gentleman.   52

    Her. So is Lysander.

    The.   In himself he is;
But, in this kind, wanting your father's voice,
The other must be held the worthier.

    Her. I would my father look'd but with my
      eyes.   56

    The. Rather your eyes must with his judgment
      look.

    Her. I do entreat your Grace to pardon me.
I know not by what power I am made bold,
Nor how it may concern my modesty   60
In such a presence here to plead my thoughts;
But I beseech your Grace that I may know
The worst that may befall me in this case,
If I refuse to wed Demetrius.   64

    The. Either to die the death, or to abjure
For ever the society of men.
Therefore, fair Hermia, question your desires;
Know of your youth, examine well your blood,   68
Whether, if you yield not to your father's choice,
You can endure the livery of a nun,
For aye to be in shady cloister mew'd,
To live a barren sister all your life,   72
Chanting faint hymns to the cold fruitless moon.
Thrice blessed they that master so their blood,
To undergo such maiden pilgrimage;
But earthlier happy is the rose distill'd,   76

51 disfigure: *destroy*   54 kind: *respect, i.e., as husband*
60 concern: *befit*   71 mew'd: *shut up*
75 pilgrimage: *the journey of life*   76 distill'd: *reduced to essence*

Than that which withering on the virgin thorn
Grows, lives, and dies, in single blessedness.

Her. So will I grow, so live, so die, my lord,
Ere I will yield my virgin patent up   80
Unto his lordship, whose unwished yoke
My soul consents not to give sovereignty.

The. Take time to pause; and, by the next new
    moon,—
The sealing-day betwixt my love and me   84
For everlasting bond of fellowship,—
Upon that day either prepare to die
For disobedience to your father's will,
Or else to wed Demetrius, as he would;   88
Or on Diana's altar to protest
For aye austerity and single life.

Dem. Relent, sweet Hermia; and Lysander, yield
Thy crazed title to my certain right.   92

Lys. You have her father's love, Demetrius;
Let me have Hermia's: do you marry him.

Ege. Scornful Lysander! true, he hath my love,
And what is mine my love shall render him;   96
And she is mine, and all my right of her
I do estate unto Demetrius.

Lys. I am, my lord, as well deriv'd as he,
As well possess'd; my love is more than his;   100
My fortunes every way as fairly rank'd,
If not with vantage, as Demetrius';
And, which is more than all these boasts can be,
I am belov'd of beauteous Hermia.   104
Why should not I then prosecute my right?
Demetrius, I'll avouch it to his head,
Made love to Nedar's daughter, Helena,

WHY

80 virgin patent: *privilege of virginity*
89 protest: *vow*   92 crazed: *unsound*
98 estate unto: *bestow upon*   100 possess'd: *endowed*

And won her soul; and she, sweet lady, dotes,
Devoutly dotes, dotes in idolatry, 109
Upon this spotted and inconstant man.

   The. I must confess that I have heard so much,
And with Demetrius thought to have spoke thereof; 112
But, being over-full of self-affairs,
My mind did lose it. But, Demetrius, come;
And come, Egeus; you shall go with me,
I have some private schooling for you both. 116
For you, fair Hermia, look you arm yourself
To fit your fancies to your father's will,
Or else the law of Athens yields you up,
Which by no means we may extenuate, 120
To death, or to a vow of single life.
Come, my Hippolyta: what cheer, my love?
Demetrius and Egeus, go along:
I must employ you in some business 124
Against our nuptial, and confer with you
Of something nearly that concerns yourselves.

   Ege. With duty and desire we follow you.

     Exeunt. Manet Lysander and Hermia.

   Lys. How now, my love! Why is your cheek so
     pale? 128
How chance the roses there do fade so fast?

   Her. Belike for want of rain, which I could well
Beteem them from the tempest of mine eyes.

   Lys. Ay me! for aught that ever I could read, 132
Could ever hear by tale or history,
The course of true love never did run smooth;
But, either it was different in blood,—

---

113 self-affairs: *my own concerns*   125 Against: *in preparation for*
126 nearly that: *that closely*
127 S. d. Manet: *(i.e., manent) remain*   131 Beteem: *grant*

Her. O cross! too high to be enthrall'd to low. 136
Lys. Or else misgraffed in respect of years,—
Her. O spite! too old to be engag'd to young.
Lys. Or else it stood upon the choice of friends,—
Her. O hell! to choose love by another's eye. 140
Lys. Or, if there were a sympathy in choice,
War, death, or sickness did lay siege to it,
Making it momentany as a sound,
Swift as a shadow, short as any dream, 144
Brief as the lightning in the collied night,
That, in a spleen, unfolds both heaven and earth,
And ere a man hath power to say, 'Behold!'
The jaws of darkness do devour it up: 148
So quick bright things come to confusion.
Her. If then true lovers have been ever cross'd,
It stands as an edict in destiny:
Then let us teach our trial patience, 152
Because it is a customary cross,
As due to love as thoughts and dreams and sighs,
Wishes and tears, poor fancy's followers.
Lys. A good persuasion: therefore, hear me,
Hermia. 156
I have a widow aunt, a dowager
Of great revenue, and she hath no child:
From Athens is her house remote seven leagues;
And she respects me as her only son. 160
There, gentle Hermia, may I marry thee,
And to that place the sharp Athenian law
Cannot pursue us. If thou lov'st me then,
Steal forth thy father's house to-morrow night,
And in the wood, a league without the town, 165
Where I did meet thee once with Helena,

137 misgraffed: *badly matched*
145 collied: *blackened*
149 confusion: *ruin*
155 fancy's: *love's*

143 momentany: *momentary*
146 spleen: *sudden fit of passion*
150 ever: *always*
160 respects: *looks upon*

To do observance to a morn of May,
There will I stay for thee.
    Her.   My good Lysander!   168
I swear to thee by Cupid's strongest bow,
By his best arrow with the golden head,
By the simplicity of Venus' doves,
By that which knitteth souls and prospers loves,
And by that fire which burn'd the Carthage
    queen,   173
When the false Troyan under sail was seen,
By all the vows that ever men have broke,—
In number more than ever women spoke,—   176
In that same place thou hast appointed me,
To-morrow truly will I meet with thee.
    Lys. Keep promise, love. Look, here comes
    Helena.

                Enter Helena.

    Her. God speed fair Helena! Whither away?   180
    Hel. Call you me fair? that fair again unsay.
Demetrius loves your fair: O happy fair!
Your eyes are lode-stars! and your tongue's sweet air
More tuneable than lark to shepherd's ear,   184
When wheat is green, when hawthorn buds appear.
Sickness is catching: O! were favour so,
Yours would I catch, fair Hermia, ere I go;
My ear should catch your voice, my eye your eye,
My tongue should catch your tongue's sweet
    melody.   189
Were the world mine, Demetrius being bated,
The rest I'll give to be to you translated.
O! teach me how you look, and with what art

173 Carthage queen: *Dido*   174 Troyan: *Æneas*
182 fair: *beauty*   183 lode-stars: *guiding-stars*
184 tuneable: *tuneful*   186 favour: *charm*
190 bated: *excepted*   191 translated: *transformed*

You sway the motion of Demetrius' heart.   193

   Her. I frown upon him, yet he loves me still.

   Hel. O! that your frowns would teach my smiles
     such skill.

   Her. I give him curses, yet he gives me love.

   Hel. O! that my prayers could such affection
     move.   197

   Her. The more I hate, the more he follows me.

   Hel. The more I love, the more he hateth me.

   Her. His folly, Helena, is no fault of mine.

   Hel. None, but your beauty: would that fault were
     mine!   201

   Her. Take comfort: he no more shall see my face;
Lysander and myself will fly this place.
Before the time I did Lysander see,   204
Seem'd Athens as a paradise to me:
O! then, what graces in my love do dwell,
That he hath turn'd a heaven unto a hell.

   Lys. Helen, to you our minds we will unfold.
To-morrow night, when Phœbe doth behold   209
Her silver visage in the wat'ry glass,
Decking with liquid pearl the bladed grass,—
A time that lovers' flights doth still conceal,—
Through Athens' gates have we devis'd to steal.

   Her. And in the wood, where often you and I
Upon faint primrose-beds were wont to lie,
Emptying our bosoms of their counsel sweet,   216
There my Lysander and myself shall meet;
And thence from Athens turn away our eyes,
To seek new friends and stranger companies.
Farewell, sweet playfellow: pray thou for us;
And good luck grant thee thy Demetrius!   221

206, 207 *Cf. n.*   209 Phœbe: *the moon*
212 still: *always*   215 faint: *pale* (?), *faintly perfumed* (?)
216 counsel: *inmost thought*

Keep word, Lysander: we must starve our sight
From lovers' food till morrow deep midnight.

Exit Hermia.

Lys. I will, my Hermia.—Helena, adieu: 224
As you on him, Demetrius dote on you!

Exit Lysander.

Hel. How happy some o'er other some can be!
Through Athens I am thought as fair as she;
But what of that? Demetrius thinks not so;   228
He will not know what all but he do know;
And as he errs, doting on Hermia's eyes,
So I, admiring of his qualities.
Things base and vile, holding no quantity,   232
Love can transpose to form and dignity.
Love looks not with the eyes, but with the mind,
And therefore is wing'd Cupid painted blind.
Nor hath Love's mind of any judgment taste;
Wings and no eyes figure unheedy haste: 237
And therefore is Love said to be a child,
Because in choice he is so oft beguil'd.
As waggish boys in game themselves forswear,
So the boy Love is perjur'd everywhere;   241
For ere Demetrius look'd on Hermia's eyne,
He hail'd down oaths that he was only mine;
And when this hail some heat from Hermia felt,
So he dissolv'd, and showers of oaths did melt.
I will go tell him of fair Hermia's flight: 246
Then to the wood will he to-morrow night
Pursue her; and for this intelligence
If I have thanks, it is a dear expense:
But herein mean I to enrich my pain,   250
To have his sight thither and back again.   *Exit.*

232, 233 *Cf. n.*   240 game: *jest*   242 eyne: *eyes*
248 intelligence: *information*   249 dear expense; *cf. n.*

$\boxed{\text{Scene Two}}$

[*A Room in Quince's House*]

*Enter Quince the Carpenter, Snug the Joiner, Bottom
the Weaver, Flute the Bellows-mender, Snout the
Tinker, and Starveling the Tailor.*

Quin. Is all our company here?

Bot. You were best to call them generally,
man by man, according to the scrip.   3

Quin. Here is the scroll of every man's name,
which is thought fit, through all Athens, to play
in our interlude before the duke and the duchess
on his wedding-day at night.   7

Bot. First, good Peter Quince, say what the
play treats on; then read the names of the
actors, and so grow to a point.   10

Quin. Marry, our play is, The most lament-
able comedy, and most cruel death of Pyramus
and Thisby.   13

Bot. A very good piece of work, I assure you,
and a merry.   Now, good Peter Quince, call
forth your actors by the scroll.   Masters, spread
yourselves.   17

Quin. Answer as I call you.   Nick Bottom,
the weaver.

Bot. Ready.   Name what part I am for, and
proceed.   21

Quin. You, Nick Bottom, are set down for
Pyramus.

Bot. What is Pyramus? a lover, or a tyrant?

Quin. A lover, that kills himself most gal-
lantly for love.   26

2 generally; *cf. n.*   3 scrip: *written paper*
11 Marry: *an oath from the name of the Virgin Mary*

Bot. That will ask some tears in the true per-
forming of it: if I do it, let the audience look to
their eyes; I will move storms, I will condole
in some measure. To the rest: yet my chief
humour is for a tyrant. I could play Ercles
rarely, or a part to tear a cat in, to make all
split.   33

   'The raging rocks
   And shivering shocks
   Shall break the locks   36
    Of prison gates:
   And Phibbus' car
   Shall shine from far
   And make and mar   40
    The foolish Fates.'

This was lofty! Now name the rest of the
players. This is Ercles' vein, a tyrant's vein; a
lover is more condoling.   44

Quin. Francis Flute, the bellows-mender.

Flu. Here, Peter Quince.

Quin. You must take Thisby on you.

Flu. What is Thisby? a wandering knight?

Quin. It is the lady that Pyramus must love.

Flu. Nay, faith, let not me play a woman; I
have a beard coming.   51

Quin. That's all one: you shall play it in a
mask, and you may speak as small as you will.

Bot. An I may hide my face, let me play
Thisby too. I'll speak in a monstrous little
voice, 'Thisne, Thisne!' 'Ah, Pyramus, my lover
dear; thy Thisby dear, and lady dear!'   57

---

31 Ercles: *Hercules*   32 tear a cat: *rant*
38 Phibbus': *Phœbus', the sun-god's*
54 An: *if*   56 Thisne; *cf. n.*

Quin. No, no; you must play Pyramus; and
Flute, you Thisby.

Bot. Well, proceed.   60

Quin. Robin Starveling, the tailor.

Star. Here, Peter Quince.

Quin. Robin Starveling, you must play Thisby's mother. Tom Snout, the tinker.   64

Snout. Here, Peter Quince.

Quin. You, Pyramus's father; myself, Thisby's father; Snug, the joiner, you the lion's part:
and, I hope, here is a play fitted.   68

Snug. Have you the lion's part written? pray
you, if it be, give it me, for I am slow of study.

Quin. You may do it extempore, for it is nothing but roaring.   72

Bot. Let me play the lion too. I will roar,
that I will do any man's heart good to hear me;
I will roar, that I will make the duke say, 'Let
him roar again, let him roar again.'   76

Quin. An you should do it too terribly, you
would fright the duchess and the ladies, that
they would shriek; and that were enough to
hang us all.   80

All. That would hang us, every mother's son.

Bot. I grant you, friends, if that you should
fright the ladies out of their wits, they would
have no more discretion but to hang us; but I
will aggravate my voice so that I will roar you
as gently as any sucking dove; I will roar you
an 'twere any nightingale.   87

Quin. You can play no part but Pyramus;
for Pyramus is a sweet-faced man; a proper
man, as one shall see in a summer's day; a

87 an 'twere: *as if it were*   89 proper: *fine, handsome*

most lovely, gentleman-like man; therefore, you
must needs play Pyramus.   92

Bot. Well, I will undertake it. What beard
were I best to play it in?

Quin. Why, what you will.   95

Bot. I will discharge it in either your straw-
colour beard, your orange-tawny beard, your
purple-in-grain beard, or your French-crown
colour beard, your perfect yellow.   99

Quin. Some of your French crowns have no
hair at all, and then you will play bare-faced.
But masters, here are your parts; and I am to
entreat you, request you, and desire you, to con
them by to-morrow night, and meet me in the 105
palace wood, a mile without the town, by moonlight: there will we rehearse; for if we meet in
the city, we shall be dogged with company, and
our devices known. In the meantime I will draw
a bill of properties, such as our play wants. I
pray you, fail me not.   110

Bot. We will meet; and there we may rehearse more obscenely and courageously. Take
pains; be perfect; adieu.

Quin. At the duke's oak we meet.

Bot. Enough; hold, or cut bow-strings.   115

Exeunt.

96 discharge: *perform*
98 purple-in-grain: *fast-dyed purple*   French-crown colour: *color of*
 a gold coin   *a gold coin*
                                               104 con: *learn by heart*
109 bill: *list*   115 *Cf. n.*

ACT SECOND

Scene One

[*A Wood near Athens*]

Enter a Fairy at one door, and Robin Goodfellow at another.

Puck. How now, spirit! whither wander you?
Fai. Over hill, over dale,
  Thorough bush, thorough brier,
 Over park, over pale,   4
  Thorough flood, thorough fire,
 I do wander everywhere,
 Swifter than the moon's sphere;
 And I serve the fairy queen,   8
 To dew her orbs upon the green:
 The cowslips tall her pensioners be;
 In their gold coats spots you see;
 Those be rubies, fairy favours,   12
  In their freckles live their savours:
I must go seek some dew-drops here,
And hang a pearl in every cowslip's ear.
Farewell, thou lob of spirits: I'll be gone;   16
Our queen and all her elves come here anon.
 Puck. The king doth keep his revels here to-night.
Take heed the queen come not within his sight;
For Oberon is passing fell and wrath,   20
Because that she as her attendant hath
A lovely boy, stol'n from an Indian king;
She never had so sweet a changeling;

Scene One S. d. at one door; *cf. n.* Robin Goodfellow; *cf. n.*
3 Thorough: *through* 4 pale: *fence* 7 moon's sphere; *cf. n.*
9 orbs; *cf. n.* 10 pensioners; *cf. n.* 12 favours: *love-tokens*
16 lob: *bumpkin* 17 anon: *presently*
20 passing fell: *exceedingly angry* wrath: *wroth*
23 changeling; *cf. n.*

And jealous Oberon would have the child   24
Knight of his train, to trace the forests wild;
But she, perforce, withholds the loved boy,
Crowns him with flowers, and makes him all her joy.
And now they never meet in grove, or green,   28
By fountain clear, or spangled starlight sheen,
But they do square; that all their elves, for fear,
Creep into acorn-cups and hide them there.

   Fai. Either I mistake your shape and making
      quite,   32
Or else you are that shrewd and knavish sprite
Call'd Robin Goodfellow: are you not he
That frights the maidens of the villagery;
Skim milk, and sometimes labour in the quern,
And bootless make the breathless housewife churn;   37
And sometime make the drink to bear no barm;
Mislead night wanderers, laughing at their harm?
Those that Hobgoblin call you and sweet Puck,
You do their work, and they shall have good luck: 41
Are you not he?
   Puck.   Fairy, thou speak'st aright;
I am that merry wanderer of the night.
I jest to Oberon, and make him smile   44
When I a fat and bean-fed horse beguile,
Neighing in likeness of a filly foal:
And sometime lurk I in a gossip's bowl,
In very likeness of a roasted crab;   48
And, when she drinks, against her lips I bob
And on her wither'd dewlap pour the ale.
The wisest aunt, telling the saddest tale,

25 trace: *traverse*   29 sheen: *bright*
30 square: *quarrel*   that: *so that*   32 making: *form*
33 shrewd: *malicious, mischievous*
36 quern: *hand-mill for grinding grain*
37 bootless: *fruitlessly*   38 barm: *froth*
47 gossip's bowl; *cf ⁓*   48 crab: *crab-apple*   51 saddest: *soberest*

Sometime for three-foot stool mistaketh me;   52
Then slip I from her bum, down topples she,
And 'tailor' cries, and falls into a cough;
And then the whole quire hold their hips and laugh;
And waxen in their mirth, and neeze, and swear   56
A merrier hour was never wasted there.
But, room, fairy! here comes Oberon.

 Fai. And here my mistress. Would that he were
  gone!

*Enter the King of Fairies [Oberon] at one door with
  his train; and the Queen [Titania] at another
  with hers.*

 Obe. Ill met by moonlight, proud Titania.   60
 Tita. What! jealous Oberon. Fairies, skip hence:
I have forsworn his bed and company.
 Obe. Tarry, rash wanton! am not I thy lord?
 Tita. Then, I must be thy lady; but I know
When thou hast stol'n away from fairy land   65
And in the shape of Corin sat all day,
Playing on pipes of corn, and versing love
To amorous Phillida. Why art thou here,   68
Come from the furthest steep of India?
But that, forsooth, the bouncing Amazon,
Your buskin'd mistress and your warrior love,
To Theseus must be wedded, and you come   72
To give their bed joy and prosperity.
 Obe. How canst thou thus for shame, Titania,
Glance at my credit with Hippolyta,
Knowing I know thy love to Theseus?   76
Didst thou not lead him through the glimmering night

54 tailor; *cf. n.*   55 quire: *company*
56 waxen: *increase*   neeze: *sneeze*   66 Corin; *cf. n.*
67 versing love: *making love-verses*   69 steep: *mountain range*
71 buskin'd: *wearing a buskin, a high-heeled hunter's boot*
25 Glance: *hint maliciously*

From Perigenia, whom he ravished?
And make him with fair Ægle break his faith,
With Ariadne, and Antiopa?   80
 Tita. These are the forgeries of jealousy:
And never, since the middle summer's spring,
Met we on hill, in dale, forest, or mead,
By paved fountain, or by rushy brook,   84
Or in the beached margent of the sea,
To dance our ringlets to the whistling wind,
But with thy brawls thou hast disturb'd our sport.
Therefore the winds, piping to us in vain,   88
As in revenge, have suck'd up from the sea
Contagious fogs; which, falling in the land,
Hath every pelting river made so proud
That they have overborne their continents: 92
The ox hath therefore stretch'd his yoke in vain,
The ploughman lost his sweat, and the green corn
Hath rotted ere his youth attain'd a beard:
The fold stands empty in the drowned field,   96
And crows are fatted with the murrion flock;
The nine men's morris is fill'd up with mud,
And the quaint mazes in the wanton green
For lack of tread are undistinguishable: 100
The human mortals want their winter here:
No night is now with hymn or carol blest:
Therefore the moon, the governess of floods,
Pale in her anger, washes all the air,   104
That rheumatic diseases do abound:

---

78 Perigenia; *cf. n.*   79, 80 Ægle . . . Antiopa; *cf. n.*
81 forgeries: *idle inventions*   82 spring: *beginning*
84 paved fountain: *spring with pebble-covered bottom*
85 margent: *margin*   86 ringlets: *circular dances*
90 Contagious: *noxious*   91 pelting: *petty*
92 continents: *boundaries*   97 murrion: *diseased*
98 nine men's morris; *cf. n.*   99 wanton: *luxuriant*
101-103 *Cf. n.*   105 rheumatic diseases: *colds, etc.*

And thorough this distemperature we see
The seasons alter: hoary-headed frosts
Fall in the fresh lap of the crimson rose,   108
And on old Hiems' thin and icy crown
An odorous chaplet of sweet summer buds
Is, as in mockery, set. The spring, the summer,
The childing autumn, angry winter, change   112
Their wonted liveries, and the mazed world,
By their increase, now knows not which is which.
And this same progeny of evil comes
From our debate, from our dissension: 116
We are their parents and original.

   Obe. Do you amend it then; it lies in you.
Why should Titania cross her Oberon?
I do but beg a little changeling boy,   120
To be my henchman.

   Tita.   Set your heart at rest;
The fairy land buys not the child of me.
His mother was a votaress of my order:
And, in the spiced Indian air, by night,   124
Full often hath she gossip'd by my side,
And sat with me on Neptune's yellow sands,
Marking the embarked traders on the flood;
When we have laugh'd to see the sails conceive
And grow big-bellied with the wanton wind;
Which she, with pretty and with swimming gait
Following,—her womb then rich with my young
    squire,—
Would imitate, and sail upon the land,   132
To fetch me trifles, and return again,
As from a voyage, rich with merchandise.

---

106 distemperature: *disorder of the winds and moon (?), ill
    humor (?)*   109 Hiems': *winter's*
112 childing: *fruitful*   113 mazed: *bewildered*
114 increase: *produce*   121 henchman: *page of honor*
123 votaress: *woman under vows*

But she, being mortal, of that boy did die;
And for her sake I do rear up her boy,   136
And for her sake I will not part with him.

   Obe. How long within this wood intend you stay?

   Tita. Perchance, till after Theseus' wedding-day.
If you will patiently dance in our round,   140
And see our moonlight revels, go with us;
If not, shun me, and I will spare your haunts.

   Obe. Give me that boy, and I will go with thee.

   Tita. Not for thy fairy kingdom. Fairies,
    away!   144
We shall chide downright, if I longer stay.

              Exeunt [Titania and her train].

   Obe. Well, go thy way: thou shalt not from this
   grove
Till I torment thee for this injury.
My gentle Puck, come hither. Thou remember'st
Since once I sat upon a promontory,   149
And heard a mermaid on a dolphin's back
Uttering such dulcet and harmonious breath,
That the rude sea grew civil at her song,   152
And certain stars shot madly from their spheres
To hear the sea-maid's music.

   Puck.   I remember.

   Obe. That very time I saw, but thou couldst not,
Flying between the cold moon and the earth,   156
Cupid all arm'd: a certain aim he took
At a fair vestal throned by the west,
And loos'd his love-shaft smartly from his bow,
As it should pierce a hundred thousand hearts;
But I might see young Cupid's fiery shaft   161
Quench'd in the chaste beams of the wat'ry moon,

145 chide: *quarrel*   147 injury: *affront*
148-169 *Cf. n.*   149 Since: *when*

And the imperial votaress passed on,
In maiden meditation, fancy-free.   164
Yet mark'd I where the bolt of Cupid fell:
It fell upon a little western flower,
Before milk-white, now purple with' love's wound,
And maidens call it Love-in-idleness.   168
Fetch me that flower; the herb I show'd thee once:
The juice of it on sleeping eyelids laid
Will make or man or woman madly dote
Upon the next live creature that it sees.   172
Fetch me this herb; and be thou here again
Ere the leviathan can swim a league.
      Puck. I'll put a girdle round about the earth
In forty minutes.   *Exit.*
      Obe.   Having once this juice,   176
I'll watch Titania when she is asleep,
And drop the liquor of it in her eyes:
The next thing then she waking looks upon,
Be it on lion, bear, or wolf, or bull,   180
On meddling monkey, or on busy ape,
She shall pursue it with the soul of love:
And ere I take this charm off from her sight,
As I can take it with another herb,   184
I'll make her render up her page to me.
But who comes here? I am invisible,
And I will overhear their conference.

                  Enter Demetrius, Helena following him.

      Dem. I love thee not, therefore pursue me not.   188
Where is Lysander and fair Hermia?
The one I'll slay, the other slayeth me.
Thou told'st me they were stol'n into this wood;
And here am I, and wood within this wood,   192

168 Love-in-idleness: *the pansy*   171 or . . . or: *either . . . or*
174 leviathan: *whale*   192 wood . . . wood: *mad . . . wood*

Because I cannot meet my Hermia.
Hence! get thee gone, and follow me no more.

Hel. You draw me, you hard-hearted adamant:
But yet you draw not iron, for my heart   196
Is true as steel: leave you your power to draw,
And I shall have no power to follow you.

Dem. Do I entice you? Do I speak you fair?
Or, rather, do I not in plainest truth   200
Tell you I do not nor I cannot love you?

Hel. And even for that do I love you the more.
I am your spaniel; and, Demetrius,
The more you beat me, I will fawn on you: 204
Use me but as your spaniel, spurn me, strike me,
Neglect me, lose me; only give me leave,
Unworthy as I am, to follow you.
What worser place can I beg in your love,   208
And yet a place of high respect with me,
Than to be used as you use your dog?

Dem. Tempt not too much the hatred of my spirit,
For I am sick when I do look on you.   212

Hel. And I am sick when I look not on you.

Dem. You do impeach your modesty too much,
To leave the city, and commit yourself
Into the hands of one that loves you not;   216
To trust the opportunity of night
And the ill counsel of a desert place
With the rich worth of your virginity.

Hel. Your virtue is my privilege: for that   220
It is not night when I do see your face,
Therefore I think I am not in the night;
Nor doth this wood lack worlds of company,
For you in my respect are all the world: 224

195 adamant: *hard stone with magnetic power*
214 impeach: *call in question*
220 for that: *because*   224 respect: *regard*

Then how can it be said I am alone,
When all the world is here to look on me?

    Dem. I'll run from thee and hide me in the brakes,
And leave thee to the mercy of wild beasts.   228

    Hel. The wildest hath not such a heart as you.
Run when you will, the story shall be chang'd;
Apollo flies, and Daphne holds the chase;
The dove pursues the griffin; the mild hind   232
Makes speed to catch the tiger: bootless speed,
When cowardice pursues and valour flies.

    Dem. I will not stay thy questions: let me go;
Or, if thou follow me, do not believe   236
But I shall do thee mischief in the wood.

    Hel. Ay, in the temple, in the town, the field,
You do me mischief. Fie, Demetrius!
Your wrongs do set a scandal on my sex.   240
We cannot fight for love, as men may do;
We should be woo'd and were not made to woo.

                   [Exit Demetrius.]

I'll follow thee and make a heaven of hell,
To die upon the hand I love so well.   *Exit.*

    Obe. Fare thee well, nymph: ere he do leave this
        grove,   245
Thou shalt fly him, and he shall seek thy love.

Enter Puck.

Hast thou the flower there? Welcome, wanderer.
    Puck. Ay, there it is.
    Obe.   I pray thee, give it me.   248
I know a bank where the wild thyme blows,
Where oxlips and the nodding violet grows
Quite over-canopied with luscious woodbine,

227 brakes: *thickets*   231 *Cf. n.*
232 griffin: *fabulous monster, half lion, half eagle*
235 stay . . . questions: *listen to thy talk*   249 blows: *blooms*

With sweet musk-roses, and with eglantine: 252
There sleeps Titania some time of the night,
Lull'd in these flowers with dances and delight;
And there the snake throws her enamell'd skin,
Weed wide enough to wrap a fairy in: 256
And with the juice of this I'll streak her eyes,
And make her full of hateful fantasies.
Take thou some of it, and seek through this grove:
A sweet Athenian lady is in love   260
With a disdainful youth: anoint his eyes;
But do it when the next thing he espies
May be the lady.   Thou shalt know the man
By the Athenian garments he hath on.   264
Effect it with some care, that he may prove
More fond on her than she upon her love.
And look thou meet me ere the first cock crow.

   Puck. Fear not, my lord, your servant shall do so.
                                          Exeunt.

Scene Two

[Another Part of the Wood]

Enter Queen of Fairies, with her train.

   Tita. Come, now a roundel and a fairy song;
Then, for the third part of a minute, hence;
Some to kill cankers in the musk-rose buds,
Some war with rere-mice for their leathern wings,   4
To make my small elves coats, and some keep back
The clamorous owl, that nightly hoots, and wonders
At our quaint spirits.   Sing me now asleep;
Then to your offices, and let me rest.   8

252 eglantine: *sweetbriar*   256 Weed: *garment*
257 streak: *stroke*   1 roundel: *dance in a circle*
4 rere-mice: *bats*   7 quaint: *pretty, dainty*   8 offices: *duties*

Fairies sing.

I.

'You spotted snakes with double tongue,
　　Thorny hedge-hogs, be not seen;
Newts, and blind-worms, do no wrong;
　　Come not near our fairy queen.'　　　　12

'Philomel, with melody,
　　Sing in our sweet lullaby;
Lulla, lulla, lullaby; lulla, lulla, lullaby:
　　Never harm,　　　　　　　　　　16
　　Nor spell, nor charm,
Come our lovely lady nigh;
So, good night, with lullaby.'

II.

'Weaving spiders come not here;
　　Hence, you long-legg'd spinners, hence!　　20
Beetles black, approach not near;
　　Worm nor snail, do no offence.

　　　Philomel, with melody, &c.'　　　　24

Fai. Hence, away! now all is well.
　　One aloof stand sentinel.

　　　　　　She sleeps. [*Exeunt Fairies.*]

Enter Oberon [*and squeezes the flower on
　　　　Titania's eyelids*].

Obe. What thou seest when thou dost wake,
Do it for thy true-love take;　　　　　　28
Love and languish for his sake:
Be it ounce, or cat, or bear,
Pard, or boar with bristled hair,

13 Philomel: *the nightingale*
30 ounce: *lynx*　　cat: *wildcat*　　　　　31 Pard: *leopard*

In thy eye that shall appear   32
When thou wak'st, it is thy dear.
Wake when some vile thing is near.   [*Exit.*]

Enter Lysander and Hermia.

Lys. Fair love, you faint with wandering in the wood;
    And to speak troth, I have forgot our way: 36
We'll rest us, Hermia, if you think it good,
    And tarry for the comfort of the day.
    Her. Be it so, Lysander: find you out a bed,
For I upon this bank will rest my head.   40
    Lys. One turf shall serve as pillow for us both;
One heart, one bed, two bosoms, and one troth.
    Her. Nay, good Lysander; for my sake, my dear,
Lie further off yet, do not lie so near.   44
    Lys. O! take the sense, sweet, of my innocence,
Love takes the meaning in love's conference.
I mean that my heart unto yours is knit,
So that but one heart we can make of it;   48
Two bosoms interchained with an oath;
So then two bosoms and a single troth.
Then by your side no bed-room me deny,
For, lying so, Hermia, I do not lie.   52
    Her. Lysander riddles very prettily:
Now much beshrew my manners and my pride,
If Hermia meant to say Lysander lied.
But, gentle friend, for love and courtesy   56
Lie further off; in human modesty,
Such separation as may well be said
Becomes a virtuous bachelor and a maid,
So far be distant; and, good night, sweet friend.
Thy love ne'er alter till thy sweet life end!   61
    Lys. Amen, amen, to that fair prayer, say I;

36 troth: *truth*   54 beshrew: *'mischief on'*

And then end life when I end loyalty!

                     [Retires a little distance.]

Here is my bed: sleep give thee all his rest!

   Her. With half that wish the wisher's eyes be
       press'd!   *They sleep.*

                Enter Puck.

   Puck. Through the forest have I gone,

       But Athenian found I none,

       On whose eyes I might approve   68

       This flower's force in stirring love.

       Night and silence! who is here?

       Weeds of Athens he doth wear:

       This is he, my master said,   72

       Despised the Athenian maid:

       And here the maiden, sleeping sound,

       On the dank and dirty ground.

       Pretty soul! she durst not lie   76

       Near this lack-love, this kill-courtesy.

       Churl, upon thy eyes I throw

       All the power this charm doth owe.

       When thou wak'st, let love forbid   80

       Sleep his seat on thy eyelid:

       So awake when I am gone;

       For I must now to Oberon.   *Exit.*

     Enter Demetrius and Helena, running.

   Hel. Stay, though thou kill me, sweet Deme-
       trius.   84

   Dem. I charge thee, hence, and do not haunt me
       thus.

   Hel. O! wilt thou darkling leave me? do not so.

   Dem. Stay, on thy peril: I alone will go.

                   Exit Demetrius.

68 approve: *test*   79 owe: *possess*   86 darkling: *in the dark*

Hel. O! I am out of breath in this fond chase.
The more my prayer, the lesser is my grace.   89
Happy is Hermia, wheresoe'er she lies;
For she hath blessed and attractive eyes.
How came her eyes so bright? Not with salt tears:
If so, my eyes are oftener wash'd than hers.   93
No, no, I am as ugly as a bear;
For beasts that meet me run away for fear;
Therefore no marvel though Demetrius   96
Do, as a monster, fly my presence thus.
What wicked and dissembling glass of mine
Made me compare with Hermia's sphery eyne?
But who is here? Lysander! on the ground!   100
Dead? or asleep? I see no blood, no wound.
Lysander, if you live, good sir, awake.

    Lys. [*Awaking.*] And run through fire I will for
     thy sweet sake.
Transparent Helena! Nature shows art,   104
That through thy bosom makes me see thy heart.
Where is Demetrius? O! how fit a word
Is that vile name to perish on my sword.

    Hel. Do not say so, Lysander; say not so.   108
What though he love your Hermia? Lord! what
     though?
Yet Hermia still loves you: then be content.

    Lys. Content with Hermia! No: I do repent
The tedious minutes I with her have spent.   112
Not Hermia, but Helena I love:
Who will not change a raven for a dove?
The will of man is by his reason sway'd,
And reason says you are the worthier maid.   116
Things growing are not ripe until their season;

88 fond: *foolish; also, loving*
89 grace: *good fortune*   99 sphery: *starry*

So I, being young, till now ripe not to reason;
And touching now the point of human skill,
Reason becomes the marshal to my will,   120
And leads me to your eyes; where I o'erlook
Love's stories written in love's richest book.

    Hel. Wherefore was I to this keen mockery
       born?   123
When at your hands did I deserve this scorn?
Is 't not enough, is 't not enough, young man,
That I did never, no, nor never can,
Deserve a sweet look from Demetrius' eye,
But you must flout my insufficiency?   128
Good troth, you do me wrong, good sooth, you do,
In such disdainful manner me to woo.
But fare you well: perforce I must confess
I thought you lord of more true gentleness.   132
O! that a lady of one man refus'd,
Should of another therefore be abus'd.   *Exit.*

    Lys. She sees not Hermia.   Hermia, sleep thou
      there;
And never mayst thou come Lysander near.   136
For, as a surfeit of the sweetest things
The deepest loathing to the stomach brings;
Or, as the heresies that men do leave
Are hated most of those they did deceive: 140
So thou, my surfeit and my heresy,
Of all be hated, but the most of me!
And, all my powers, address your love and might
To honour Helen, and to be her knight.   *Exit.*

    Her. [*Awaking.*] Help me, Lysander, help me! do
      thy best   145
To pluck this crawling serpent from my breast.
Ay me, for pity! what a dream was here!

119 point: *summit*

Lysander, look how I do quake with fear: 148
Methought a serpent eat my heart away,
And you sat smiling at his cruel prey.
Lysander! what! remov'd?—Lysander! lord!
What! out of hearing? gone? no sound, no word?   152
Alack! where are you? speak, an if you hear;
Speak, of all loves! I swound almost with fear.
No! then I well perceive you are not nigh:
Either death or you I'll find immediately.   *Exit.*

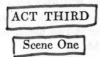

ACT THIRD

Scene One

[*The Wood.   Titania lying asleep*]

Enter the Clowns [*Quince, Snug, Bottom, Flute, Snout, and Starveling*].

Bot. Are we all met?

Quin. Pat, pat; and here's a marvellous convenient place for our rehearsal. This green plot shall be our stage, this hawthorn-brake our   4
tiring-house; and we will do it in action as we will do it before the duke.

Bot. Peter Quince,—

Quin. What sayst thou, bully Bottom?   8

Bot. There are things in this comedy of Pyramus and Thisby that will never please. First, Pyramus must draw a sword to kill himself, which the ladies cannot abide. How answer you that?   13

150 prey: *preying*   154 of: *for the sake of*   swound: *swoon*
Scene One S. d. Clowns: *men of the lower class; also, comedians*
5 tiring-house: *dressing-room*
8 bully: *a friendly term equivalent to 'good old'*

Snout. By 'r lakin, a parlous fear.

Star. I believe we must leave the killing out, when all is done.   16

Bot. Not a whit: I have a device to make all well. Write me a prologue; and let the prologue seem to say, we will do no harm with our swords, and that Pyramus is not killed indeed; and, 20 for the more better assurance, tell them that I, Pyramus, am not Pyramus, but Bottom the weaver: this will put them out of fear.

Quin. Well, we will have such a prologue, and it shall be written in eight and six.   25

Bot. No, make it two more: let it be written in eight and eight.

Snout. Will not the ladies be afeard of the lion?   29

Star. I fear it, I promise you.

Bot. Masters, you ought to consider with yourselves: to bring in,—God shield us!—a lion among ladies, is a most dreadful thing; for there is not a more fearful wild-fowl than your lion living, and we ought to look to it.

Snout. Therefore, another prologue must tell he is not a lion.   37

Bot. Nay, you must name his name, and half his face must be seen through the lion's neck; and he himself must speak through, saying thus, or to the same defect, 'Ladies,' or, 'Fair ladies,' 'I would wish you,' or, 'I would request you,' or, 42 'I would entreat you, not to fear, not to tremble: my life for yours. If you think I come hither as a lion, it were pity of my life: no, I am no such thing: I am a man as other men are'; and there

14 By 'r lakin: *By Our Lady*   parlous: *perilous*
25 eight and six: *alternate verses of eight and six syllables*

indeed let him name his name, and tell them
plainly he is Snug the joiner. 48

Quin. Well, it shall be so. But there is two
hard things, that is, to bring the moonlight
into a chamber; for you know, Pyramus and
Thisby meet by moonlight. 52

Snug. Doth the moon shine that night we
play our play?

Bot. A calendar, a calendar! look in the
almanac; find out moonshine, find out moonshine. 57

Quin. Yes, it doth shine that night.

Bot. Why, then may you leave a casement
of the great chamber-window, where we play,
open; and the moon may shine in at the casement. 62

Quin. Ay; or else one must come in with a
bush of thorns and a lantern, and say he comes
to disfigure, or to present, the person of Moonshine. Then, there is another thing: we must
have a wall in the great chamber; for Pyramus
and Thisby, says the story, did talk through the
chink of a wall. 69

Snug. You can never bring in a wall. What
say you, Bottom?

Bot. Some man or other must present Wall;
and let him have some plaster, or some loam, or
some rough-cast about him, to signify wall; and
let him hold his fingers thus, and through that
cranny shall Pyramus and Thisby whisper. 76

Quin. If that may be, then all is well. Come,
sit down, every mother's son, and rehearse your
parts. Pyramus, you begin: when you have

64 bush of thorns; *cf. n.*

spoken your speech, enter into that brake; and
so every one according to his cue.   81

Enter Robin [*behind*].

Puck. What hempen home-spuns have we swagger-
ing here,
So near the cradle of the fairy queen?
What! a play toward; I'll be an auditor;   84
An actor too perhaps, if I see cause.

  Quin. Speak, Pyramus.—Thisby, stand forth.

Bot. Thisby, the flowers of odious savours sweet,—

  Quin. Odorous, odorous.   88

Bot. —odours savours sweet:
So hath thy breath, my dearest Thisby dear.
But hark, a voice! stay thou but here awhile,
And by and by I will to thee appear.—   *Exit.*

  Puck. —A stranger Pyramus than e'er play'd here!
                                                   [*Exit.*]

  Flu. Must I speak now?

  Quin. Ay, marry, must you; for you must
understand, he goes but to see a noise that he
heard, and is to come again.   97

Flu. Most radiant Pyramus, most lily-white of hue,
Of colour like the red rose on triumphant brier,
Most brisky juvenal, and eke most lovely Jew,
As true as truest horse that yet would never
tire,   101
I'll meet thee, Pyramus, at Ninny's tomb.

  Quin. 'Ninus' tomb,' man. Why, you must
not speak that yet; that you answer to Pyramus: you speak all your part at once, cues and
all. Pyramus, enter: your cue is past; it is
'never tire.'

---

82 hempen home-spuns: *rude fellows*   84 toward: *in preparation*
100 juvenal: *an affected word for 'youth'*   eke: *also*

Flu. O!—As true as truest horse, that yet would
never tire.   108

[*Enter Puck, and Bottom with an ass's head.*]

Bot. If I were fair, Thisby, I were only thine.

Quin. O monstrous! O strange! we are haunted.
Pray, masters! fly, masters!—Help!

                                        The Clowns all exeunt.

Puck. I'll follow you, I'll lead you about a round, 112
  Through bog, through bush, through brake, through
    brier:
Sometime a horse I'll be, sometime a hound,
  A hog, a headless bear, sometime a fire;
And neigh, and bark, and grunt, and roar, and
    burn,   116
Like horse, hound, hog, bear, fire, at every turn.

                                                Exit.

  Bot. Why do they run away? this is a knavery
of them to make me afeard.

                        Enter Snout.

  Snout. O Bottom, thou art changed! what do
I see on thee?   121

  Bot. What do you see? you see an ass-head
of your own, do you?   [*Exit Snout.*]

                    Enter Peter Quince.

  Quin. Bless thee, Bottom! bless thee! thou
art translated.   *Exit.*

  Bot. I see their knavery: this is to make an
ass of me; to fright me, if they could. But I will 127
not stir from this place, do what they can: I
will walk up and down here, and I will sing,
that they shall hear I am not afraid.

115 fire: *will o' the wisp*   122, 123 you . . . own; *cf. n.*

'The ousel-cock, so black of hue,
  With orange-tawny bill,   132
The throstle with his note so true,
  The wren with little quill.'

  Tita. [*Awaking.*] What angel wakes me from
my flowery bed?   136

  Bot.   'The finch, the sparrow, and the lark,
              The plain-song cuckoo gray,
            Whose note full many a man doth mark,
              And dares not answer, nay;'   140

for indeed, who would set his wit to so foolish a
bird? who would give a bird the lie, though he
cry 'cuckoo' never so?
  Tita. I pray thee, gentle mortal, sing again:
Mine ear is much enamour'd of thy note;   145
So is mine eye enthralled to thy shape;
And thy fair virtue's force, perforce, doth move me,
On the first view, to say, to swear, I love thee.
  Bot. Methinks, mistress, you should have 149
little reason for that: and yet, to say the truth,
reason and love keep little company together
now-a-days. The more the pity, that some
honest neighbours will not make them friends.
Nay, I can gleek upon occasion.   154
  Tita. Thou art as wise as thou art beautiful.
  Bot. Not so, neither; but if I had wit enough
to get out of this wood, I have enough to serve
mine own turn.
  Tita. Out of this wood do not desire to go:
Thou shalt remain here, whether thou wilt or no.
I am a spirit of no common rate;   161

131 ousel-cock: *male blackbird*   134 quill: *note*
138 plain-song; *cf. n.*   154 gleek: *jest*

The summer still doth tend upon my state;
And I do love thee: therefore, go with me;
I'll give thee fairies to attend on thee,   164
And they shall fetch thee jewels from the deep,
And sing, while thou on pressed flowers dost sleep:
And I will purge thy mortal grossness so
That thou shalt like an airy spirit go.   168
Pease-blossom! Cobweb! Moth! and Mustard-seed!

Enter four Fairies.

  Peas. Ready.
  Cob.   And I.
  Moth.   And I.
  Mus.   And I.
  All Four.   Where shall we go?
  Tita. Be kind and courteous to this gentleman;
Hop in his walks, and gambol in his eyes;   172
Feed him with apricocks and dewberries,
With purple grapes, green figs, and mulberries.
The honey-bags steal from the humble-bees,
And for night-tapers crop their waxen thighs,   176
And light them at the fiery glow-worm's eyes,
To have my love to bed, and to arise;
And pluck the wings from painted butterflies
To fan the moonbeams from his sleeping eyes: 180
Nod to him, elves, and do him courtesies.
    Peas. Hail, mortal!
    Cob. Hail!
    Moth. Hail!   184
    Mus. Hail!
    Bot. I cry your worships mercy, heartily: I
beseech your worship's name.
    Cob. Cobweb.   188

169 Moth; *cf. n.*   186 cry . . . mercy: *beg . . . pardon*

Bot. I shall desire you of more acquaintance, good Master Cobweb: if I cut my finger, I shall make bold with you. Your name, honest gentleman?   192

Peas. Pease-blossom.

Bot. I pray you, commend me to Mistress Squash, your mother, and to Master Peascod, your father. Good Master Pease-blossom, I shall desire you of more acquaintance too. Your name, I beseech you, sir?   198

Mus. Mustard-seed.

Bot. Good Master Mustard-seed, I know your patience well: that same cowardly, giant-like ox-beef hath devoured many a gentleman of 202 your house. I promise you, your kindred hath made my eyes water ere now. I desire you of more acquaintance, good Master Mustard-seed.

Tita. Come, wait upon him; lead him to my
bower.   206
The moon, methinks, looks with a watery eye;
And when she weeps, weeps every little flower,
Lamenting some enforced chastity.
Tie up my love's tongue, bring him silently.   210

Exeunt.

Scene Two

[*Another Part of the Wood*]

Enter King of Fairies, solus.

Obe. I wonder if Titania be awak'd;
Then, what it was that next came in her eye,
Which she must dote on in extremity.

195 Squash: *unripe peapod*   Peascod: *peapod*
209 enforced: *violated*

Enter Puck.

Here comes my messenger.

                    How now, mad spirit! 4
What night-rule now about this haunted grove?
  Puck. My mistress with a monster is in love.
Near to her close and consecrated bower,
While she was in her dull and sleeping hour, 8
A crew of patches, rude mechanicals,
That work for bread upon Athenian stalls,
Were met together to rehearse a play
Intended for great Theseus' nuptial day. 12
The shallowest thick-skin of that barren sort,
Who Pyramus presented in their sport,
Forsook his scene, and enter'd in a brake:
When I did him at this advantage take, 16
An ass's nowl I fixed on his head:
Anon his Thisbe must be answered,
And forth my mimick comes. When they him spy,
As wild geese that the creeping fowler eye, 20
Or russet-pated choughs, many in sort,
Rising and cawing at the gun's report,
Sever themselves, and madly sweep the sky;
So, at his sight, away his fellows fly, 24
And, at our stamp, here o'er and o'er one falls;
He murder cries, and help from Athens calls.
Their sense thus weak, lost with their fears thus
      strong, 27
Made senseless things begin to do them wrong;
For briers and thorns at their apparel snatch;

---

5 night-rule: *diversion of the night*   haunted: *much frequented*
7 close: *secret*
9 patches: *clowns, fools*   mechanicals: *workingmen*
13 barren sort: *dull company*   17 nowl: *noddle, pate*
21 russet-pated: *grey-headed*   choughs: *jackdaws*
25 our stamp; *cf. n.*

Some sleeves, some hats, from yielders all things
    catch.
I led them on in this distracted fear,
And left sweet Pyramus translated there;   32
When in that moment, so it came to pass,
Titania wak'd and straightway lov'd an ass.

    Obe. This falls out better than I could devise.
But hast thou yet latch'd the Athenian's eyes   36
With the love-juice, as I did bid thee do?

    Puck. I took him sleeping,—that is finish'd too,—
And the Athenian woman by his side;
That, when he wak'd, of force she must be ey'd.   40

Enter Demetrius and Hermia.

    Obe. Stand close: this is the same Athenian.
    Puck. This is the woman; but not this the man.
    Dem. O! why rebuke you him that loves you so?
Lay breath so bitter on your bitter foe.   44

    Her. Now I but chide; but I should use thee worse,
For thou, I fear, hast given me cause to curse.
If thou hast slain Lysander in his sleep,
Being o'er shoes in blood, plunge in the deep,
And kill me too.   49
The sun was not so true unto the day
As he to me. Would he have stol'n away
From sleeping Hermia? I'll believe as soon   52
This whole earth may be bor'd, and that the moon
May through the centre creep, and so displease
Her brother's noontide with the Antipodes.
It cannot be but thou hast murder'd him;   56
So should a murderer look, so dead, so grim.

    Dem. So should the murder'd look, and so should I,
Pierc'd through the heart with your stern cruelty;

36 latch'd: *moistened (?)*   40 force: *necessity*   55 with: *among*

Yet you, the murderer, look as bright, as clear,
As yonder Venus in her glimmering sphere.   61

   Her. What's this to my Lysander? where is he?
Ah! good Demetrius, wilt thou give him me?

   Dem. I had rather give his carcass to my
     hounds.   64

   Her. Out, dog! out, cur! thou driv'st me past the
     bounds
Of maiden's patience. Hast thou slain him then?
Henceforth be never number'd among men!
O! once tell true, tell true, e'en for my sake;   68
Durst thou have look'd upon him being awake,
And hast thou kill'd him sleeping? O brave touch!
Could not a worm, an adder, do so much?
An adder did it; for with doubler tongue   72
Than thine, thou serpent, never adder stung.

   Dem. You spend your passion on a mispris'd mood:
I am not guilty of Lysander's blood,
Nor is he dead, for aught that I can tell.   76

   Her. I pray thee, tell me then that he is well.

   Dem. An if I could, what should I get therefore?

   Her. A privilege never to see me more.
And from thy hated presence part I so;   80
See me no more, whether he be dead or no.   *Exit.*

   Dem. There is no following her in this fierce vein:
Here therefore for awhile I will remain.
So sorrow's heaviness doth heavier grow   84
For debt that bankrupt sleep doth sorrow owe;
Which now in some slight measure it will pay,
If for his tender here I make some stay.   *Lie down.*

   Obe. What hast thou done? thou hast mistaken
     quite,   88
And laid the love-juice on some true-love's sight:

70 touch: *exploit*   71 worm: *snake*
74 on a mispris'd mood: *in a mistaken anger (?)*   87 tender: *offer*

Of thy misprision must perforce ensue
Some true-love turn'd, and not a false turn'd true.

    Puck. Then fate o'er-rules, that, one man holding troth,   **92**
A million fail, confounding oath on oath.

    Obe. About the wood go swifter than the wind,
And Helena of Athens look thou find:
All fancy-sick she is, and pale of cheer   **96**
With sighs of love, that costs the fresh blood dear.
By some illusion see thou bring her here:
I'll charm his eyes against she do appear.

    Puck. I go, I go; look how I go;   **100**
Swifter than arrow from the Tartar's bow.   *Exit.*

    Obe.   Flower of this purple dye,
       Hit with Cupid's archery,
       Sink in apple of his eye.   **104**
       When his love he doth espy,
       Let her shine as gloriously
       As the Venus of the sky.
       When thou wak'st, if she be by,   **108**
       Beg of her for remedy.

Enter Puck.

    Puck.   Captain of our fairy band,
       Helena is here at hand,
       And the youth, mistook by me,   **112**
       Pleading for a lover's fee.   *FOOLISH*
       Shall we their fond pageant see?
       Lord, what fools these mortals be!

    Obe.   Stand aside: the noise they make   **116**
       Will cause Demetrius to awake.

    Puck. Then will two at once woo one;

---

90 misprision: *mistake*   **96** cheer: *face*
97 costs . . . dear; *cf. n.*
99 against: *in expectation of the time when*

That must needs be sport alone;
And those things do best please me   120
That befall preposterously.

Enter Lysander and Helena.

Lys. Why should you think that I should woo in
    scorn?
  Scorn and derision never come in tears:
Look, when I vow, I weep; and vows so born,
  In their nativity all truth appears.   125
How can these things in me seem scorn to you,
Bearing the badge of faith to prove them true?
Hel. You do advance your cunning more and
    more.   128
  When truth kills truth, O devilish-holy fray!
These vows are Hermia's: will you give her o'er?
  Weigh oath with oath, and you will nothing weigh:
Your vows, to her and me, put in two scales,   132
Will even weigh, and both as light as tales.
    Lys. I had no judgment when to her I swore.
    Hel. Nor none, in my mind, now you give her o'er.
    Lys. Demetrius loves her, and he loves not
    you.   136
    Dem. [*Awaking.*] O Helen! goddess, nymph, per-
    fect, divine!
To what, my love, shall I compare thine eyne?
Crystal is muddy. O! how ripe in show   139
Thy lips, those kissing cherries, tempting grow;
This pure congealed white, high Taurus' snow,
Fann'd with the eastern wind, turns to a crow
When thou hold'st up thy hand. O! let me kiss
This princess of pure white, this seal of bliss.   144

119 alone: *having no equal*
125 *By their birth appear wholly true*   129 *Cf. n.*
141 Taurus': *lofty mountain range in Asiatic Turkey*

Hel. O spite! O hell! I see you all are bent
To set against me for your merriment:
If you were civil and knew courtesy,
You would not do me thus much injury.   148
Can you not hate me, as I know you do,
But you must join in souls to mock me too?
If you were men, as men you are in show,
You would not use a gentle lady so;   152
To vow, and swear, and superpraise my parts,
When I am sure you hate me with your hearts.
You both are rivals, and love Hermia,
And now both rivals, to mock Helena: 156
A trim exploit, a manly enterprise,
To conjure tears up in a poor maid's eyes
With your derision! none of noble sort
Would so offend a virgin, and extort   160
A poor soul's patience, all to make you sport.

Lys. You are unkind, Demetrius; be not so;
For you love Hermia; this you know I know:
And here, with all good will, with all my heart,
In Hermia's love I yield you up my part: 165
And yours of Helena to me bequeath,
Whom I do love, and will do to my death.

Hel. Never did mockers waste more idle breath.

Dem. Lysander, keep thy Hermia; I will none:
If e'er I lov'd her, all that love is gone.
My heart to her but as guest-wise sojourn'd,
And now to Helen it is home return'd,   172
There to remain.

Lys.   Helen, it is not so.

Dem. Disparage not the faith thou dost not know,
Lest to thy peril thou aby it dear.
Look! where thy love comes: yonder is thy dear.

157 trim: *fine*   160 extort: *wrest away*
175 aby: *pay a penalty for*

Enter Hermia.

Her. Dark night, that from the eye his function
    takes,   177
The ear more quick of apprehension makes;
Wherein it doth impair the seeing sense,
It pays the hearing double recompense.   180
Thou art not by mine eye, Lysander, found;
Mine ear, I thank it, brought me to thy sound.
But why unkindly didst thou leave me so?

    Lys. Why should he stay, whom love doth press
      to go?   184

    Her. What love could press Lysander from my
      side?

    Lys. Lysander's love, that would not let him bide,
Fair Helena, who more engilds the night
Than all yon fiery oes and eyes of light.   188
Why seek'st thou me? could not this make thee know,
The hate I bare thee made me leave thee so?

    Her. You speak not as you think: it cannot be.

    Hel. Lo! she is one of this confederacy.   192
Now I perceive they have conjoin'd all three
To fashion this false sport in spite of me.
Injurious Hermia! most ungrateful maid!
Have you conspir'd, have you with these con-
    triv'd   196
To bait me with this foul derision?
Is all the counsel that we two have shar'd,
The sisters' vows, the hours that we have spent,
When we have chid the hasty-footed time   200
For parting us, O! is all forgot?
All school-days' friendship, childhood innocence?
We, Hermia, like two artificial gods,

---

188 oes: *small circular spangles; also, o's*   194 spite: *contempt*
195 Injurious: *insulting*   203 artificial: *skilled in constructive a*

Have with our needles created both one flower,   204
Both on one sampler, sitting on one cushion,
Both warbling of one song, both in one key,
As if our hands, our sides, voices, and minds,
Had been incorporate. So we grew together,   208
Like to a double cherry, seeming parted,
But yet an union in partition;
Two lovely berries moulded on one stem;
So, with two seeming bodies, but one heart;   212
Two of the first, like coats in heraldry,
Due but to one, and crowned with one crest.
And will you rent our ancient love asunder,
To join with men in scorning your poor friend?
It is not friendly, 'tis not maidenly: 217
Our sex, as well as I, may chide you for it,
Though I alone do feel the injury.

    Her. I am amazed at your passionate words.
I scorn you not: it seems that you scorn me.

    Hel. Have you not set Lysander, as in scorn,
To follow me and praise my eyes and face,
And made your other love, Demetrius,—   224
Who even but now did spurn me with his foot,—
To call me goddess, nymph, divine and rare,
Precious, celestial? Wherefore speaks he this
To her he hates? and wherefore doth Lysander
Deny your love, so rich within his soul,   229
And tender me, forsooth, affection,
But by your setting on, by your consent?
What though I be not so in grace as you,   232
So hung upon with love, so fortunate,
But miserable most, to love unlov'd?
This you should pity rather than despise.

    Her. I understand not what you mean by this.   236

211 lovelv: *loving*   213, 214 *Cf. n.*   215 rent: *rend*

Hel. Ay, do, persever, counterfeit sad looks,
Make mouths upon me when I turn my back;
Wink each at other; hold the sweet jest up:
This sport, well carried, shall be chronicled. 240
If you have any pity, grace, or manners,
You would not make me such an argument.
But, fare ye well: 'tis partly mine own fault,
Which death or absence soon shall remedy. 244

Lys. Stay, gentle Helena! hear my excuse:
My love, my life, my soul, fair Helena!

Hel. O excellent!

Her.   Sweet, do not scorn her so.

Dem. If she cannot entreat, I can compel. 248

Lys. Thou canst compel no more than she entreat:
Thy threats have no more strength than her weak
        prayers.
Helen, I love thee; by my life, I do:
I swear by that which I will lose for thee, 252
To prove him false that says I love thee not.

Dem. I say I love thee more than he can do.

Lys. If thou say so, withdraw, and prove it too.

Dem. Quick, come!

Her.   Lysander, whereto tends all this?

Lys. Away, you Ethiop!

Dem.   No, no, he'll . . . 257
Seem to break loose; take on, as you would follow,
But yet come not: you are a tame man, go!

Lys. [*To Hermia.*] Hang off, thou cat, thou burr!
        vile thing, let loose, 260
Or I will shake thee from me like a serpent.

Her. Why are you grown so rude? what change
        is this?
Sweet love,—

237 sad: *serious*   239 hold . . . up: *carry . . . on*
242 argument: *subject (of merriment)*   257 *Cf. n.*

Lys.   Thy love! out, tawny Tartar, out!
Out, loathed medicine! hated potion, hence!   264
  Her. Do you not jest?
  Hel.   Yes, sooth; and so do you.
  Lys. Demetrius, I will keep my word with thee.
  Dem. I would I had your bond, for I perceive
A weak bond holds you: I'll not trust your word.
  Lys. What! should I hurt her, strike her, kill her
      dead?   269
Although I hate her, I'll not harm her so.
  Her. What! can you do me greater harm than hate?
Hate me! wherefore?   O me! what news, my
      love?   272
Am not I Hermia?   Are not you Lysander?
I am as fair now as I was erewhile.
Since night you lov'd me; yet, since night you left me:
Why, then you left me,—O, the gods forbid!—
In earnest, shall I say?
  Lys.   Ay, by my life;   277
And never did desire to see thee more.
Therefore be out of hope, of question, doubt;
Be certain, nothing truer: 'tis no jest,   280
That I do hate thee and love Helena.
  Her. O me! you juggler! you canker-blossom!
You thief of love! what! have you come by night
And stol'n my love's heart from him?
  Hel.   Fine, i' faith!
Have you no modesty, no maiden shame,   285
No touch of bashfulness?   What! will you tear
Impatient answers from my gentle tongue?
Fie, fie! you counterfeit, you puppet you!   288
  Her. Puppet! why, so: ay, that way goes the game.
Now I perceive that she hath made compare

282 canker-blossom: *worm that destroys the blossom*

Between our statures: she hath urg'd her height;
And with her personage, her tall personage,   292
Her height, forsooth, she hath prevail'd with him.
And are you grown so high in his esteem,
Because I am so dwarfish and so low?
How low am I, thou painted maypole? speak;
How low am I? I am not yet so low   297
But that my nails can reach unto thine eyes.

   Hel. I pray you, though you mock me, gentlemen,
Let her not hurt me: I was never curst;   300
I have no gift at all in shrewishness;
I am a right maid for my cowardice:
Let her not strike me. You perhaps may think,
Because she is something lower than myself,   304
That I can match her.

   Her.   Lower! hark, again.

   Hel. Good Hermia, do not be so bitter with me.
I evermore did love you, Hermia,
Did ever keep your counsels, never wrong'd you;
Save that, in love unto Demetrius,   309
I told him of your stealth unto this wood.
He follow'd you; for love I follow'd him;
But he hath chid me hence, and threaten'd me
To strike me, spurn me, nay, to kill me too: 313
And now, so you will let me quiet go,
To Athens will I bear my folly back,
And follow you no further: let me go: 316
You see how simple and how fond I am.

   Her. Why, get you gone. Who is 't that hinders
    you?

   Hel. A foolish heart, that I leave here behind.

   Her. What! with Lysander?

292 personage: *figure*
302 right: *real*

            300 curst: *savage*
      304 something: *somewhat*

Hel.   With Demetrius.

Lys. Be not afraid: she shall not harm thee,
    Helena.   321

Dem. No, sir; she shall not, though you take her
    part.

Hel. O! when she's angry, she is keen and shrewd.
She was a vixen when she went to school: 324
And though she be but little, she is fierce.

Her. 'Little' again! nothing but 'low' and 'little'!
Why will you suffer her to flout me thus?
Let me come to her.

    Lys.   Get you gone, you dwarf;   328
You minimus, of hindering knot-grass made;
You bead, you acorn!

    Dem.   You are too officious
In her behalf that scorns your services.
Let her alone; speak not of Helena;   332
Take not her part, for, if thou dost intend
Never so little show of love to her,
Thou shalt aby it.

    Lys.   Now she holds me not;
Now follow, if thou dar'st, to try whose right,
Or thine or mine, is most in Helena.   337

Dem. Follow! nay, I'll go with thee, cheek by jole.
              Exeunt Lysander and Demetrius.

Her. You, mistress, all this coil is long of you:
Nay, go not back.

    Hel.   I will not trust you, I,   340
Nor longer stay in your curst company.
Your hands than mine are quicker for a fray,
My legs are longer though, to run away.   [*Exit.*]

329 minimus: *diminutive creature*   hindering knot-grass; *cf. n.*
333 intend: *pretend*   338 jole: *jaw*
339 coil: *turmoil*   long of: *because of*

Her. I am amaz'd, and know not what to say.

                                                      [Exit.]

  Obe. This is thy negligence: still thou mis-
    tak'st,   345
Or else commit'st thy knaveries wilfully.

  Puck. Believe me, king of shadows, I mistook.
Did not you tell me I should know the man   348
By the Athenian garments he had on?
And so far blameless proves my enterprise,
That I have 'nointed an Athenian's eyes;
And so far am I glad it so did sort,   352
As this their jangling I esteem a sport.

  Obe. Thou see'st these lovers seek a place to fight:
Hie therefore, Robin, overcast the night;
The starry welkin cover thou anon   356
With drooping fog as black as Acheron;
And lead these testy rivals so astray,
As one come not within another's way.
Like to Lysander sometime frame thy tongue,
Then stir Demetrius up with bitter wrong;   361
And sometime rail thou like Demetrius;
And from each other look thou lead them thus,
Till o'er their brows death-counterfeiting sleep
With leaden legs and batty wings doth creep:
Then crush this herb into Lysander's eye;
Whose liquor hath this virtuous property,
To take from thence all error with his might,   368
And make his eyeballs roll with wonted sight.
When they next wake, all this derision
Shall seem a dream and fruitless vision;
And back to Athens shall the lovers wend,   372
With league whose date till death shall never end.

---

352 sort: *turn out*   357 Acheron: *one of the rivers of Hades*
361 wrong: *insult*   367 virtuous: *powerful*
368 with his might: *by its efficacy*

Whiles I in this affair do thee employ,
I'll to my queen and beg her Indian boy;
And then I will her charmed eye release   376
From monster's view, and all things shall be peace.

   Puck. My fairy lord, this must be done with haste,
For night's swift dragons cut the clouds full fast,
And yonder shines Aurora's harbinger;   380
At whose approach, ghosts, wandering here and there,
Troop home to churchyards: damned spirits all,
That in cross-ways and floods have burial,
Already to their wormy beds are gone;   384
For fear lest day should look their shames upon,
They wilfully themselves exile from light,
And must for aye consort with black-brow'd night.

   Obe. But we are spirits of another sort.   388
I with the morning's love have oft made sport;
And, like a forester, the groves may tread,
Even till the eastern gate, all fiery-red,
Opening on Neptune, with fair blessed beams   392
Turns into yellow gold his salt green streams.
But, notwithstanding, haste; make no delay:
We may effect this business yet ere day.

                                [Exit Oberon.]

   Puck. Up and down, up and down;   396
       I will lead them up and down:
       I am fear'd in field and town;
       Goblin, lead them up and down.
Here comes one.   400

          Enter Lysander.

   Lys. Where art thou, proud Demetrius? speak thou
   now.
   Puck. Here, villain! drawn and ready. Where art
   thou?

389 the morning's love; *cf. n.*   402 drawn: *with drawn sword*

Lys. I will be with thee straight.

Puck.   Follow me, then,
To plainer ground.

[*Exit Lysander as following the voice.*]

Enter Demetrius.

Dem.   Lysander! speak again.   404
Thou runaway, thou coward, art thou fled?
Speak! In some bush? Where dost thou hide thy
  head?

Puck. Thou coward! art thou bragging to the stars,
Telling the bushes that thou look'st for wars,
And wilt not come? Come, recreant; come, thou
  child;   409
I'll whip thee with a rod: he is defil'd
That draws a sword on thee.

Dem.   Yea, art thou there?

Puck. Follow my voice: we'll try no manhood here.
Exeunt.

[*Enter Lysander.*]

Lys. He goes before me and still dares me on:
When I come where he calls, then he is gone.
The villain is much lighter-heel'd than I:
I follow'd fast, but faster he did fly;   416
That fallen am I in dark uneven way,
And here will rest me.   *Lie down.*
                    Come, thou gentle day!
For if but once thou show me thy grey light,
I'll find Demetrius and revenge this spite.   420

[*Sleeps.*]

Enter Robin and Demetrius.

Puck. Ho! ho! ho! Coward, why com'st thou not?

Dem. Abide me, if thou dar'st; for well I wot

Thou runn'st before me, shifting every place,
And dar'st not stand, nor look me in the face.
Where art thou now?

    Puck.   Come hither: I am here.

    Dem. Nay then, thou mock'st me. Thou shalt buy
       this dear,

If ever I thy face by daylight see:

Now, go thy way. Faintness constraineth me   428

To measure out my length on this cold bed:

By day's approach look to be visited.

                    [Lies down and sleeps.]

Enter Helena.

Hel. O weary night! O long and tedious night,

    Abate thy hours! shine, comforts, from the
       east!   432

That I may back to Athens by daylight,

    From these that my poor company detest:

And sleep, that sometimes shuts up sorrow's eye,

Steal me awhile from mine own company.   436

                              Sleep.

    Puck. Yet but three? Come one more;

            Two of both kinds make up four.

            Here she comes, curst and sad:

            Cupid is a knavish lad,   440

            Thus to make poor females mad.

Enter Hermia.

Her. Never so weary, never so in woe,

    Bedabbled with the dew and torn with briers,

I can no further crawl, no further go;   444

    My legs can keep no pace with my desires.

Here will I rest me till the break of day.

432 Abate: *shorten*

Heavens shield Lysander, if they mean a fray!

                     [*Lies down and sleeps.*]

Puck.	On the ground 448
	Sleep sound:
	I'll apply
	To your eye,

Gentle lover, remedy.   452

        [*Squeezing the juice on Lysander's eyes.*]

             When thou wak'st,

             Thou tak'st

             True delight

             In the sight   456

Of thy former lady's eye:

And the country proverb known,

That every man should take his own,

In your waking shall be shown: 460

             Jack shall have Jill;

             Nought shall go ill;

The man shall have his mare again,

And all shall be well.   [*Exit Puck.*]

             They sleep all the Act.

ACT FOURTH

Scene One

[*The Same*]

Enter Queen of Fairies and Clown and Fairies, and
       the King behind them [*unseen*].

Tita. Come, sit thee down upon this flowery bed,

  While I thy amiable cheeks do coy,

And stick musk-roses in thy sleek smooth head,

---

464 S. d. Act: *intermission*   2 amiable: *lovely*   coy: *caress*

And kiss thy fair large ears, my gentle joy.   4

Bot. Where's Pease-blossom?

Peas. Ready.

Bot. Scratch my head, Pease-blossom. Where's
Mounsieur Cobweb?   8

Cob. Ready.

Bot. Mounsieur Cobweb, good mounsieur, get
your weapons in your hand, and kill me a red-
hipped humble-bee on the top of a thistle; and,
good mounsieur, bring me the honey-bag. Do
not fret yourself too much in the action, mounsieur; and, good mounsieur, have a care the
honey-bag break not; I would be loath to have
you overflown with a honey-bag, signior. Where's
Mounsieur Mustard-seed?   18

Must. Ready.

Bot. Give me your neaf, Mounsieur Mustard-
seed. Pray you, leave your courtesy, good
mounsieur.

Must. What's your will?   23

Bot. Nothing, good mounsieur, but to help
Cavalery Cobweb to scratch. I must to the
barber's, mounsieur, for methinks I am marvellous hairy about the face; and I am such a
tender ass, if my hair do but tickle me, I must
scratch.   29

Tita. What, wilt thou hear some music, my sweet
love?

Bot. I have a reasonable good ear in music:
let us have the tongs and the bones.   33

Tita. Or say, sweet love, what thou desir'st to eat.

Bot. Truly, a peck of provender: I could

20 neaf: *fist*   21 leave your courtesy: *omit formality*
25 Cavalery: *i.e., cavalier*
33 the tongs and the bones: *rude musical instruments*

munch your good dry oats.   Methinks I have
a great desire to a bottle of hay: good hay, sweet
hay, hath no fellow.   39

Tita. I have a venturous fairy that shall seek
The squirrel's hoard, and fetch thee thence new nuts.

Bot. I had rather have a handful or two of
dried pease.   But, I pray you, let none of your
people stir me: I have an exposition of sleep
come upon me.   45

Tita. Sleep thou, and I will wind thee in my arms.
Fairies, be gone, and be all ways away.

> *[Exeunt Fairies.]*

So doth the woodbine the sweet honeysuckle   48
Gently entwist; the female ivy so
Enrings the barky fingers of the elm.
O! how I love thee; how I dote on thee!

> *[They sleep.]*

Enter Robin Goodfellow.

Obe. *[Advancing.]* Welcome, good Robin.   See'st
  thou this sweet sight?   52
Her dotage now I do begin to pity:
For, meeting her of late behind the wood,
Seeking sweet favours for this hateful fool,
I did upbraid her and fall out with her;   56
For she his hairy temples then had rounded
With coronet of fresh and fragrant flowers;
And that same dew, which sometime on the buds
Was wont to swell like round and orient pearls, 60
Stood now within the pretty flowerets' eyes
Like tears that did their own disgrace bewail.
When I had at my pleasure taunted her,
And she in mild terms begg'd my patience,   64

38 bottle: *bundle*   55 favours: *flowers as gifts*
60 orient: *lustrous*

I then did ask of her her changeling child;
Which straight she gave me, and her fairy sent
To bear him to my bower in fairy land.
And now I have the boy, I will undo   68
This hateful imperfection of her eyes:
And, gentle Puck, take this transformed scalp
From off the head of this Athenian swain,
That, he awaking when the other do,   72
May all to Athens back again repair,
And think no more of this night's accidents
But as the fierce vexation of a dream.
But first I will release the fairy queen.   76

             [Touching her eyes with an herb.]

   Be as thou wast wont to be;
   See as thou wast wont to see:
   Dian's bud o'er Cupid's flower
   Hath such force and blessed power.   80
Now, my Titania; wake you, my sweet queen.
   Tita. My Oberon! what visions have I seen!
Methought I was enamour'd of an ass.
   Obe. There lies your love.
   Tita.   How came these things to pass?
O! how mine eyes do loathe his visage now.   85
   Obe. Silence a while. Robin, take off this head.
Titania, music call; and strike more dead
Than common sleep of all these five the sense.
   Tita. Music, ho! music! such as charmeth sleep.
                            Music, still.
   Puck. When thou wak'st, with thine own fool's
     eyes peep.
   Obe. Sound, music! Come, my queen, take hands
     with me,

And rock the ground whereon these sleepers be.
Now thou and I are new in amity,   93
And will to-morrow midnight solemnly
Dance in Duke Theseus' house triumphantly,
And bless it to all fair prosperity.   96
There shall the pairs of faithful lovers be
Wedded, with Theseus, all in jollity.

  Puck. Fairy king, attend, and mark:
      I do hear the morning lark.   100

  Obe. Then, my queen, in silence sad,
      Trip we after the night's shade;
      We the globe can compass soon,
      Swifter than the wandering moon.   104

  Tita. Come, my lord; and in our flight
      Tell me how it came this night
      That I sleeping here was found
      With these mortals on the ground.   108

Sleepers lie still. Exeunt [Fairies]. Wind Horns.

Enter Theseus, Hippolyta, Egeus, and all his train.

  The. Go, one of you, find out the forester;
For now our observation is perform'd;
And since we have the vaward of the day,
My love shall hear the music of my hounds.   112
Uncouple in the western valley; let them go:
Dispatch, I say, and find the forester.
We will, fair queen, up to the mountain's top,
And mark the musical confusion   116
Of hounds and echo in conjunction.

  Hip. I was with Hercules and Cadmus once,
When in a wood of Crete they bay'd the bear
With hounds of Sparta: never did I hear   120

95 triumphantly: *festively*   108 S. d. Wind: *blow*
110 observation: *observance of the rites of May Day*
111 vaward: *early part*   113 Uncouple: *unleash them*
114 Dispatch: *make haste*   119 bay'd: *brought to bay*

Such gallant chiding; for, besides the groves,
The skies, the fountains, every region near
Seem'd all one mutual cry. I never heard
So musical a discord, such sweet thunder.   124
    The. My hounds are bred out of the Spartan kind,
So flew'd, so sanded; and their heads are hung
With ears that sweep away the morning dew;   127
Crook-knee'd, and dew-lapp'd like Thessalian bulls;
Slow in pursuit, but match'd in mouth like bells,
Each under each. A cry more tuneable
Was never holla'd to, nor cheer'd with horn,
In Crete, in Sparta, nor in Thessaly: 132
Judge, when you hear. But, soft! what nymphs are
    these?
    Ege. My lord, this is my daughter here asleep;
And this, Lysander; this Demetrius is;
This Helena, old Nedar's Helena: 136
I wonder of their being here together.
    The. No doubt they rose up early to observe
The rite of May, and, hearing our intent,
Came here in grace of our solemnity.   140
But speak, Egeus, is not this the day
That Hermia should give answer of her choice?
    Ege. It is, my lord.
    The. Go, bid the huntsmen wake them with their
    horns.   144

                    Horns and they wake. Shout within.
                                    They all start up.

Good morrow, friends. Saint Valentine is past:
Begin these wood-birds but to couple now?
    Lys. Pardon, my lord.
    The.   I pray you all, stand up.

121 chiding: *noise (of hounds)*
126 flew'd: *having large chaps*   sanded: *of a sandy color*
129 mouth: *voice*   bells: *i.e., a chime of bells*   133 soft: *stop*
140 in grace of: *i.e., to grace*   145 Saint Valentine; *cf. n.*

I know you two are rival enemies: 148
How comes this gentle concord in the world,
That hatred is so far from jealousy,
To sleep by hate, and fear no enmity?

   Lys. My lord, I shall reply amazedly, 152
Half sleep, half waking: but as yet, I swear,
I cannot truly say how I came here;
But, as I think,—for truly would I speak,
And now I do bethink me, so it is,— 156
I came with Hermia hither: our intent
Was to be gone from Athens, where we might,
Without the peril of the Athenian law—

   Ege. Enough, enough, my lord; you have
    enough: 160
I beg the law, the law, upon his head.
They would have stol'n away; they would, Demetrius,
Thereby to have defeated you and me;
You of your wife, and me of my consent, 164
Of my consent that she should be your wife.

   Dem. My lord, fair Helen told me of their stealth,
Of this their purpose hither, to this wood;
And I in fury hither follow'd them, 168
Fair Helena in fancy following me.
But, my good lord, I wot not by what power,—
But by some power it is,—my love to Hermia,
Melted as the snow, seems to me now 172
As the remembrance of an idle gawd
Which in my childhood I did dote upon;
And all the faith, the virtue of my heart,
The object and the pleasure of mine eye, 176
Is only Helena. To her, my lord,
Was I betroth'd ere I saw Hermia:
But, like a sickness, did I loathe this food;

150 jealousy: *suspicion*   159 Without: *beyond*

But, as in health, come to my natural taste,
Now do I wish it, love it, long for it,   181
And will for evermore be true to it.

　　The. Fair lovers, you are fortunately met:
Of this discourse we more will hear anon.   184
Egeus, I will overbear your will,
For in the temple, by and by, with us,
These couples shall eternally be knit:
And, for the morning now is something worn,
Our purpos'd hunting shall be set aside.   189
Away with us, to Athens: three and three,
We'll hold a feast in great solemnity.
Come, Hippolyta.   192

　　　　　Exit Duke [with Hippolyta] and Lords.

　　Dem. These things seem small and undistinguish-
　　　　able,
Like far-off mountains turned into clouds.

　　Her. Methinks I see these things with parted eye,
When everything seems double.

　　Hel.　　　　　　　　　So methinks:
And I have found Demetrius, like a jewel,   197
Mine own, and not mine own.

　　Dem.　　　　　　　　　　Are you sure
That we are awake? It seems to me
That yet we sleep, we dream. Do you not think
The duke was here, and bid us follow him?   201

　　Her. Yea: and my father.

　　Hel.　　　　　　　And Hippolyta.

　　Lys. And he did bid us follow to the temple.

　　Dem. Why then, we are awake. Let's follow
　　　　him;   204
And by the way let us recount our dreams.

　　　　　　　　　　　　　　　　　Exeunt Lovers.

195 parted eye: *i.e., the two eyes not in focus*   197, 198 *Cf. n.*

Bottom wakes.

Bot. When my cue comes, call me, and
I will answer: my next is, 'Most fair Pyramus.' Heigh-ho! Peter Quince! Flute, the
bellows-mender! Snout, the tinker! Starveling!
God's my life! stolen hence, and left me asleep!
I have had a most rare vision. I have had a 211
dream, past the wit of man to say what dream
it was: man is but an ass, if he go about to ex-
pound this dream. Methought I was—there is
no man can tell what. Methought I was,—and
methought I had,—but man is but a patched
fool, if he will offer to say what methought I had.
The eye of man hath not heard, the ear of man 218
hath not seen, man's hand is not able to taste,
his tongue to conceive, nor his heart to report,
what my dream was. I will get Peter Quince to
write a ballad of this dream: it shall be called
Bottom's Dream, because it hath no bottom;
and I will sing it in the latter end of a play,
before the duke: peradventure, to make it the
more gracious, I shall sing it at her death.   226
                                          Exit.

Scene Two

[*A Room in Quince's House*]

Enter Quince, Flute, Snout, and Starveling.

Quin. Have you sent to Bottom's house? is
he come home yet?

216 patched: *motley*
226 gracious: *acceptable*   at her death; *cf. n.*

Star. He cannot be heard of. Out of doubt
he is transported.   4

Flu. If he come not, then the play is marred:
it goes not forward, doth it?

Quin. It is not possible: you have not a man
in all Athens able to discharge Pyramus but
he.   9

Flu. No; he hath simply the best wit of any
handicraft man in Athens.

Quin. Yea, and the best person too; and he
is a very paramour for a sweet voice.   13

Flu. You must say, 'paragon': a paramour
is, God bless us! a thing of naught.

Enter Snug the Joiner.

Snug. Masters, the duke is coming from the
temple, and there is two or three lords and ladies
more married: if our sport had gone forward,
we had all been made men.   19

Flu. O sweet bully Bottom! Thus hath he lost
sixpence a day during his life; he could not have
'scaped sixpence a day: an the duke had not
given him sixpence a day for playing Pyramus,
I'll be hanged; he would have deserved it: sixpence a day in Pyramus, or nothing.   25

Enter Bottom.

Bot. Where are these lads? where are these
hearts?

Quin. Bottom! O most courageous day! O
most happy hour!   29

Bot. Masters, I am to discourse wonders: but
ask me not what; for if I tell you, I am no true

4 transported: *transformed (?)*
15 a thing of naught: *something wicked*   27 hearts: *good fellows*

Athenian. I will tell you everything, right as it
fell out.   33

Quin. Let us hear, sweet Bottom.

Bot. Not a word of me. All that I will tell
you is, that the duke hath dined. Get your apparel together, good strings to your beards, new
ribbons to your pumps; meet presently at the
palace; every man look o'er his part; for the
short and the long is, our play is preferred. In 40
any case, let Thisby have clean linen; and let
not him that plays the lion pare his nails, for
they shall hang out for the lion's claws. And,
most dear actors, eat no onions nor garlic, for
we are to utter sweet breath, and I do not doubt
but to hear them say, it is a sweet comedy. No 46
more words: away! go; away!   *Exeunt.*

[handwritten margin note: WORDS + MIND FAIL TO ACCEPT REALITY]

ACT FIFTH

Scene One

[The Palace of Theseus]

Enter Theseus, Hippolyta, [Philostrate,] and Lords.

Hip. 'Tis strange, my Theseus, that these lovers
    speak of.

The. More strange than true. I never may believe
These antic fables, nor these fairy toys.
Lovers and madmen have such seething brains,
Such shaping fantasies, that apprehend   5
More than cool reason ever comprehends.
The lunatic, the lover, and the poet,

[handwritten margin notes: IMAGINATION; WHO SEES THE TRUE WORLD?]

40 preferred: *accepted (?), offered for acceptance (by the duke) (?)*
3 antic: *fantastic* toys: *trifling tales* 5 apprehend: *perceive*

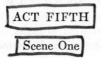

[handwritten note: ALL PRODUCE ILLUSIONS]

Are of imagination all compact: 8
One sees more devils than vast hell can hold,
That is the madman; the lover, all as frantic,
Sees Helen's beauty in a brow of Egypt:
The poet's eye, in a fine frenzy rolling,   12
Doth glance from heaven to earth, from earth to
    heaven;
And, as imagination bodies forth
The forms of things unknown, the poet's pen
Turns them to shapes, and gives to airy nothing   16
A local habitation and a name.
Such tricks hath strong imagination,
That, if it would but apprehend some joy,
It comprehends some bringer of that joy;   20
Or in the night, imagining some fear,
How easy is a bush suppos'd a bear!

    Hip. But all the story of the night told over,
And all their minds transfigur'd so together,   24
More witnesseth than fancy's images,
And grows to something of great constancy,
But, howsoever, strange and admirable.

    Enter lovers, Lysander, Demetrius, Hermia, and
            Helena.

    The. Here come the lovers, full of joy and
    mirth.   28
Joy, gentle friends! joy, and fresh days of love
Accompany your hearts!
    Lys. More than to us
Wait in your royal walks, your board, your bed!
    The. Come now; what masques, what dances shall
    we have,   32

8 compact: *composed*
11 Helen: *Helen of Troy*   brow of Egypt: *gypsy's face*
19, 20 *Cf. n.*   25 More witnesseth: *is evidence of more*
26 constancy: *consistency*   27 admirable: *to be wondered at*

To wear away this long age of three hours
Between our after-supper and bed-time?
Where is our usual manager of mirth?
What revels are in hand?   Is there no play,   36
To ease the anguish of a torturing hour?
Call Philostrate.
    Philost.   Here, mighty Theseus.
    The. Say, what abridgment have you for this even-
       ing?
What masque? what music? How shall we beguile   40
The lazy time, if not with some delight?
    Philost. There is a brief how many sports are ripe;
Make choice of which your highness will see first.
                          [Gives a paper.]
    The. 'The battle with the Centaurs, to be sung   44
By an Athenian eunuch to the harp.'
We'll none of that: that have I told my love,
In glory of my kinsman Hercules.
'The riot of the tipsy Bacchanals,   48
Tearing the Thracian singer in their rage.'
That is an old device; and it was play'd
When I from Thebes came last a conqueror.
'The thrice three Muses mourning for the death
Of Learning, late deceas'd in beggary.'   53
That is some satire keen and critical,
Not sorting with a nuptial ceremony.
'A tedious brief scene of young Pyramus   56
And his love Thisbe; very tragical mirth.'
Merry and tragical! tedious and brief!
That is, hot ice and wondrous strange snow.
How shall we find the concord of this discord?

---

34 after-supper: *dessert*   39 abridgment: *pastime*
49 Thracian singer: *Orpheus*
50 device: *something devised for dramatic representation*
54 critical: *censorious*   55 sorting with: *befitting*

Philost. A play there is, my lord, some ten words
    long,   61
Which is as brief as I have known a play;
But by ten words, my lord, it is too long,
Which makes it tedious; for in all the play   64
There is not one word apt, one player fitted.
And tragical, my noble lord, it is;
For Pyramus therein doth kill himself.

WHEN?

Which when I saw rehears'd, I must confess,   68
Made mine eyes water; but more merry tears
The passion of loud laughter never shed.
   The. What are they that do play it?
   Philost. Hard-handed men, that work in Athens
    here,   72
Which never labour'd in their minds till now,
And now have toil'd their unbreath'd memories
With this same play, against your nuptial.
   The. And we will hear it.
   Philost.   No, my noble lord;
It is not for you: I have heard it over,   77
And it is nothing, nothing in the world;
Unless you can find sport in their intents,
Extremely stretch'd and conn'd with cruel pain,
To do you service.
   The.   I will hear that play;   81
For never anything can be amiss,
When simpleness and duty tender it.
Go, bring them in: and take your places, ladies.
                       [*Exit Philostrate.*]
   Hip. I love not to see wretchedness o'er-
    charg'd,   85
And duty in his service perishing.

74 unbreath'd: *unpractised*   79, 80 intents . . . conn'd; *cf. n.*
85 o'ercharg'd: *overburdened*

The. Why, gentle sweet, you shall see no such
  thing.

Hip. He says they can do nothing in this kind. 88

The. The kinder we, to give them thanks for nothing.

Our sport shall be to take what they mistake:
And what poor duty cannot do, noble respect
Takes it in might, not merit. 92

Where I have come, great clerks have purposed
To greet me with premeditated welcomes;
Where I have seen them shiver and look pale,
Make periods in the midst of sentences, 96
Throttle their practis'd accent in their fears,
And, in conclusion, dumbly have broke off,
Not paying me a welcome. Trust me, sweet,
Out of this silence yet I pick'd a welcome; 100
And in the modesty of fearful duty
I read as much as from the rattling tongue
Of saucy and audacious eloquence.
Love, therefore, and tongue-tied simplicity 104
In least speak most, to my capacity.

[*Enter Philostrate.*]

Philost. So please your Grace, the Prologue is
  address'd.

The. Let him approach.

  Flour[*ish of*] *Trum*[*pets*].

Enter the Prologue (*Quince*).

Prol. If we offend, it is with our good will.
  That you should think, we come not to offend, 109
But with good will. To show our simple skill,
  That is the true beginning of our end.

92 *I.e., takes the will for the deed*   93 clerks: *scholars*
105 capacity: *understanding*   106 address'd: *ready*
107 S. d. Flourish: *blast*

Consider then we come but in despite.   112
  We do not come as minding to content you,
Our true intent is. All for your delight,
  We are not here. That you should here repent you,
The actors are at hand; and, by their show,   116
You shall know all that you are like to know.

    The. This fellow doth not stand upon points.

    Lys. He hath rid his prologue like a rough
colt; he knows not the stop. A good moral, my
lord: it is not enough to speak, but to speak
true.   122

    Hip. Indeed he hath played on his prologue
like a child on a recorder; a sound, but not in
government.

    The. His speech was like a tangled chain;
nothing impaired, but all disordered. Who is
next?   128

Enter Pyramus and Thisbe, Wall, Moonshine, and
    Lion, Tawyer with a trumpet before them.

Prol. Gentles, perchance you wonder at this show;
  But wonder on, till truth make all things plain.
This man is Pyramus, if you would know;
  This beauteous lady Thisby is, certain.   132
This man, with lime and rough-cast, doth present
  Wall, that vile Wall which did these lovers sunder;
And through Wall's chink, poor souls, they are con-
    tent   135
  To whisper, at the which let no man wonder.
This man, with lantern, dog, and bush of thorn,
  Presenteth Moonshine; for, if you will know,
By moonshine did these lovers think no scorn

---

118 stand upon points: *pun on senses 'mind punctuation' and 'be*
    over-careful'
120 stop: *both 'period' and 'method of stopping a horse'*
124 recorder: *wind instrument of flute type*   128 S. d. Tawyer; *cf.* **n.**

To meet at Ninus' tomb, there, there to woo.   140
This grisly beast, which Lion hight by name,
The trusty Thisby, coming first by night,
Did scare away, or rather did affright;
And, as she fled, her mantle she did fall,   144
  Which Lion vile with bloody mouth did stain.
Anon comes Pyramus, sweet youth and tall,
  And finds his trusty Thisby's mantle slain:
Whereat, with blade, with bloody blameful blade, 148
  He bravely broach'd his boiling bloody breast;
And Thisby, tarrying in mulberry shade,
  His dagger drew, and died. For all the rest,
Let Lion, Moonshine, Wall, and lovers twain,   152
At large discourse, while here they do remain.

                           Exeunt all but Wall.

   The. I wonder, if the lion be to speak.
   Dem. No wonder, my lord: one lion may,
when many asses do.   156
   Wall. In this same interlude it doth befall
That I, one Snout by name, present a wall;
And such a wall, as I would have you think,
That had in it a crannied hole or chink,   160
Through which the lovers, Pyramus and Thisby,
Did whisper often very secretly.
This loam, this rough-cast, and this stone doth show
That I am that same wall; the truth is so;   164
And this the cranny is, right and sinister,
Through which the fearful lovers are to whisper.
   The. Would you desire lime and hair to speak
better?   168
   Dem. It is the wittiest partition that ever I
heard discourse, my lord.
   The. Pyramus draws near the wall: silence!

141 hight: *is called*   144 fall: *let fall*
146 tall: *goodly*   165 sinister: *left*

Enter Pyramus.

Pyr. O grim-look'd night! O night with hue so
    black!   172
O night which ever art when day is not!
O night! O night! alack, alack, alack!
I fear my Thisby's promise is forgot.
And thou, O wall! O sweet, O lovely wall!   176
    That stand'st between her father's ground and
    mine;
Thou wall, O wall! O sweet, and lovely wall!
    Show me thy chink to blink through with mine eyne.
                  [Wall holds up his fingers.]
Thanks, courteous wall: Jove shield thee well for
    this!   180
    But what see I? No Thisby do I see.
O wicked wall! through whom I see no bliss;
    Curs'd be thy stones for thus deceiving me!
    The. The wall, methinks, being sensible,
should curse again.   185
    Pyr. No, in truth, sir, he should not. 'De-
ceiving me,' is Thisby's cue: she is to enter now,
and I am to spy her through the wall. You
shall see, it will fall pat as I told you. Yonder
she comes.

Enter Thisbe.

This. O wall! full often hast thou heard my moans,
    For parting my fair Pyramus and me: 192
My cherry lips have often kiss'd thy stones,
    Thy stones with lime and hair knit up in thee.
Pyr. I see a voice: now will I to the chink,
    To spy an I can hear my Thisby's face.   196
Thisby!

184 sensible: *capable of perception*   189 fall: *happen*

This. My love! thou art my love, I think.

Pyr. Think what thou wilt, I am thy lover's grace;
And, like Limander, am I trusty still.   200

This. And I like Helen, till the Fates me kill.

Pyr. Not Shafalus to Procrus was so true.

This. As Shafalus to Procrus, I to you.

Pyr. O! kiss me through the hole of this vile wall.

This. I kiss the wall's hole, not your lips at all.

Pyr. Wilt thou at Ninny's tomb meet me straightway?

This. 'Tide life, 'tide death, I come without delay.

Wall. Thus have I, Wall, my part discharged so;   208
And, being done, thus Wall away doth go.

> *Exeunt Clowns.*

The. Now is the mural down between the two neighbours.

Dem. No remedy, my lord, when walls are so wilful to hear without warning.   213

Hip. This is the silliest stuff that ever I heard.

The. The best in this kind are but shadows, and the worst are no worse, if imagination amend them.   217

Hip. It must be your imagination then, and not theirs.

The. If we imagine no worse of them than they of themselves, they may pass for excellent men.   Here come two noble beasts in, a man and a lion.

Enter Lion and Moonshine.

Lion. You, ladies, you, whose gentle hearts do fear   224
The smallest monstrous mouse that creeps on floor,

199 lover's grace: *i.e., lover*   200 Limander; *cf. n.*
207 'Tide: *come*   210 mural: *wall; cf. n.*

May now perchance both quake and tremble here,
　When lion rough in wildest rage doth roar.
Then know that I, one Snug the joiner, am　　228
A lion-fell, nor else no lion's dam:
For, if I should as lion come in strife
Into this place, 'twere pity on my life.

　　The. A very gentle beast, and of a good conscience.　　233

　　Dem. The very best at a beast, my lord, that e'er I saw.

　　Lys. This lion is a very fox for his valour.

　　The. True; and a goose for his discretion.　　237

　　Dem. Not so, my lord; for his valour cannot carry his discretion, and the fox carries the goose.　　240

　　The. His discretion, I am sure, cannot carry his valour, for the goose carries not the fox. It is well: leave it to his discretion, and let us listen to the moon.　　244

Moon. This lanthorn doth the horned moon present;—

　　Dem. He should have worn the horns on his head.

　　The. He is no crescent, and his horns are invisible within the circumference.　　249

Moon. This lanthorn doth the horned moon present;
Myself the man i' the moon do seem to be.

　　The. This is the greatest error of all the rest. The man should be put into the lantern: how is it else the man i' the moon?

　　Dem. He dares not come there for the candle; for, you see, it is already in snuff.　　252

229 lion-fell: *lion's skin*　　246 horns; *cf. n.*　　255 for: *because of*
256 in snuff: *with a pun on the sense 'in hasty anger'*

Hip. I am aweary of this moon: would he would change!

The. It appears, by his small light of discretion, that he is in the wane; but yet, in courtesy, in all reason, we must stay the time.   261

Lys. Proceed, Moon.

Moon. All that I have to say, is, to tell you that the lanthorn is the moon; I, the man in the moon; this thorn-bush, my thorn-bush; and this dog, my dog.

Dem. Why, all these should be in the lantern; for all these are in the moon. But, silence! here comes Thisbe.   269

Enter Thisbe.

This. This is old Ninny's tomb. Where is my love?

Lion. Oh—.   *The Lion roars; Thisbe runs off.*

Dem. Well roared, Lion.   272

The. Well run, Thisbe.

Hip. Well shone, Moon. Truly, the moon shines with a good grace.

[*The Lion tears Thisbe's mantle, and exit.*]

The. Well moused, Lion.   276

Dem. And then came Pyramus.

Lys. And so the lion vanished.

Enter Pyramus.

Pyr. Sweet moon, I thank thee for thy sunny beams;
  I thank thee, moon, for shining now so bright,
For, by thy gracious, golden, glittering beams,
  I trust to taste of truest Thisby's sight.
        But stay, O spite!
        But mark, poor knight,   284
    What dreadful dole is here!

261 stay: *await*   276 moused: *torn (as a cat tears a mouse)*

         Eyes, do you see?

         How can it be?

    O dainty duck! O dear!   288

         Thy mantle good,

         What! stain'd with blood!

    Approach, ye Furies fell!

         O Fates, come, come,

         Cut thread and thrum;

    Quail, crush, conclude, and quell!   294

  The. This passion, and the death of a dear
friend, would go near to make a man look sad.

  Hip.   Beshrew my heart, but I pity the man.

Pyr. O! wherefore, Nature, didst thou lions frame?

Since lion vile hath here deflower'd my dear?

Which is—no, no—which was the fairest dame

  That liv'd, that lov'd, that lik'd, that look'd with
    cheer.   301

         Come tears, confound;

         Out, sword, and wound

         The pap of Pyramus: 304

         Ay, that left pap,

         Where heart doth hop:

    Thus die I, thus, thus, thus.

                    [Stabs himself.]

         Now am I dead,   308

         Now am I fled;

    My soul is in the sky:

         Tongue, lose thy light!

         Moon, take thy flight!   312

                  [Exit Moonshine.]

    Now die, die, die, die, die.

---

293 thread and thrum: *the warp and its fastening, i.e., everything*
294 Quail: *overpower*   quell: *kill*
295 passion: *violent expression of sorrow*

Dem. No die, but an ace, for him; for he is
but one.

Lys. Less than an ace, man, for he is dead;
he is nothing.   317

The. With the help of a surgeon, he might
yet recover, and prove an ass.

Hip. How chance Moonshine is gone before
Thisbe comes back and finds her lover?   321

The. She will find him by starlight. Here
she comes; and her passion ends the play.

Enter Thisbe.

Hip. Methinks she should not use a long one
for such a Pyramus: I hope she will be brief.   325

Dem. A mote will turn the balance, which Pyramus, which Thisbe, is the better: he for a man,
God warrant us; she for a woman, God bless us.

Lys. She hath spied him already with those
sweet eyes.   330

Dem. And thus she moans, *videlicet:*—
This.   Asleep, my love?
             What, dead, my dove?
      O Pyramus, arise!
             Speak, speak! Quite dumb?
             Dead, dead! A tomb   336
      Must cover thy sweet eyes.
             These lily lips,
             This cherry nose,
      These yellow cowslip cheeks,   340
             Are gone, are gone:
             Lovers, make moan!
      His eyes were green as leeks.

314 No . . . ace; *cf. n.*
326, 327 which . . . which: *whether . . . or*
328 warrant: *defend*

O, Sisters Three,   344
Come, come to me,
With hands as pale as milk;
Lay them in gore,
Since you have shore   348
With shears his thread of silk.
Tongue, not a word:
Come, trusty sword:
Come, blade, my breast imbrue: 352
                            [*Stabs herself.*]
And farewell, friends;
Thus Thisby ends:
Adieu, adieu, adieu.

The. Moonshine and Lion are left to bury the
dead.   357

Dem. Ay, and Wall too.

Bot. No, I assure you; the wall is down that
parted their fathers. Will it please you to see
the epilogue, or to hear a Bergomask dance
between two of our company?   362

The. No epilogue, I pray you; for your play
needs no excuse. Never excuse; for when the
players are all dead, there need none to be
blamed. Marry, if he that writ it had played
Pyramus, and hanged himself in Thisbe's gar-
ter, it would have been a fine tragedy: and
so it is, truly, and very notably discharged.
But come, your Bergomask: let your epilogue
alone.   [*Here a dance of clowns.*]

The iron tongue of midnight hath told twelve;
Lovers, to bed; 'tis almost fairy time.   373
I fear we shall out-sleep the coming morn,

344 Sisters Three: *the three Fates*   352 imbrue: *stain with blood*
361 Bergomask dance: *a rustic dance originating in Italy*

As much as we this night have overwatch'd.
This palpable-gross play hath well beguil'd   376
The heavy gait of night. Sweet friends, to bed.
A fortnight hold we this solemnity,
In nightly revels, and new jollity.   [*Exeunt.*]

Enter Puck.

Puck. Now the hungry lion roars,   380
          And the wolf behowls the moon;
       Whilst the heavy ploughman snores,
          All with weary task fordone.
       Now the wasted brands do glow,   384
          Whilst the screech-owl, screeching loud,
       Puts the wretch that lies in woe
          In remembrance of a shroud.
       Now it is the time of night   388
          That the graves, all gaping wide,
       Every one lets forth his sprite,
          In the church-way paths to glide:
       And we fairies, that do run   392
          By the triple Hecate's team,
       From the presence of the sun,
          Following darkness like a dream,
       Now are frolic; not a mouse   396
       Shall disturb this hallow'd house:
       I am sent with broom before,
       To sweep the dust behind the door.

Enter King and Queen of Fairies, with their train.

Obe. Through the house give glimmering light
          By the dead and drowsy fire;   401
       Every elf and fairy sprite
          Hop as light as bird from brier;

---

375 overwatch'd: *overwaked*   376 palpable-gross: *stupid*
383 fordone: *exhausted*   393 *Cf. n.*   396 frolic: *merry*

	And this ditty after me	404
	Sing and dance it trippingly.	
Tita.	First, rehearse your song by rote,	
	To each word a warbling note:	
	Hand in hand, with fairy grace,	408
	Will we sing, and bless this place.	

[*Song and dance.*]

Obe.	Now, until the break of day,	
	Through this house each fairy stray.	
	To the best bride-bed will we,	412
	Which by us shall blessed be;	
	And the issue there create	
	Ever shall be fortunate.	
	So shall all the couples three	416
	Ever true in loving be;	
	And the blots of Nature's hand	
	Shall not in their issue stand:	
	Never mole, hare-lip, nor scar,	420
	Nor mark prodigious, such as are	
	Despised in nativity,	
	Shall upon their children be.	
	With this field-dew consecrate,	424
	Every fairy take his gait,	
	And each several chamber bless,	
	Through this palace, with sweet peace;	
	Ever shall in safety rest,	428
	And the owner of it blest.	
	Trip away;	
	Make no stay;	
	Meet me all by break of day.	432

[*Exeunt King, Queen, and train.*]

Puck. If we shadows have offended,

414 create: *created*   424 field-dew consecrate: *i.e., fairy holy water*
428 Ever shall: *i.e., ever shall it; cf. n.*

Think but this, and all is mended,
That you have but slumber'd here
While these visions did appear.   436
And this weak and idle theme,
No more yielding but a dream,
Gentles, do not reprehend:
If you pardon, we will mend.   440
And, as I'm an honest Puck,
If we have unearned luck
Now to 'scape the serpent's tongue,
We will make amends ere long;   444
Else the Puck a liar call:
So, good night unto you all.
Give me your hands, if we be friends,
And Robin shall restore amends.   /   [*Exit.*]

447 hands: *applause*

FINIS.

MYSTERY OF ILLUSION & REALITY.

BLEND OF ART & LIFE.

ROBIN ALSO MEANS PHALLUS.

NOTES

I. i. 5, 6. The passage of time seems as slow to Theseus as to a young man under the guardianship of a stepmother or to one who is kept from the enjoyment of his estate by his father's widow who lingers on in possession of a life-interest therein.

I. i. 31. *feigning . . . feigning.* The two words 'fain' and 'feign' were often spelled alike in the sixteenth century. Hence 'feigning' may have here its modern sense or it may mean 'love-sick,' 'yearning.' A third possibility, which I am inclined to accept, is that by 'feigning voice' Egeus means 'a repressed voice,' i.e., that Lysander sang softly so as to avoid unwelcome attention.

I. i. 32. *stol'n . . . fantasy.* 'Secretly and without permission stamped your image upon her imagination.'

I. i. 206, 207. 'How powerful must be the graces of my beloved one, seeing that they have made Athens a place of torture for me; i.e., since so long as she remained in it she could not marry Lysander.' (Deighton.)

I. i. 232, 233. 'Love, forgetting proportionate values, can so transform things base and vile that they take on form and dignity.'

I. i. 249. *dear expense.* Helena seems to mean that she will pay dearly for Demetrius' thanks—if indeed she receives them—because she will be assisting him to pursue her rival.

I. ii. 2. *generally.* Bottom obviously means just the opposite of this, i.e., separately. His intended meaning is usually fairly clear, but it would be a foolhardy editor who should attempt to translate 'Bottomese' too precisely. Cf. 'obscenely' in line 112 of this scene.

I. ii. 56. *Thisne.* This word may mean 'in this way' (in which case it should be written without a capital), or it may represent Bottom's first attempt to say Thisbe in a 'monstrous little voice.'

I. ii. 115. *hold, or cut bow-strings.* 'This phrase is of the proverbial kind, and was born in the days of archery: when a party was made at butts [archery], assurance of meeting was given in the words of that phrase; the sense of the person using them being that he would "hold" or keep promise, or they might "cut his bowstrings," demolish him for an archer.' (Capell.) This explanation is not certain, but the phrase undoubtedly means, 'Be there without fail.'

II. i. S. d. *at one door.* This refers to one of the side doors on the Elizabethan stage, and not, of course, to the imagined locality.

Robin Goodfellow. This is the proper name of the character referred to indiscriminately in the old copies as Robin or Puck. The latter was often used in the sixteenth century as a generic name for a kind of sprite or goblin. Nash, in his *Terrors of the Night* (1594), says that such mischievous beings 'did most of their merry prankes in the Night. Then ground they malt, and had hempen shirts for their labours, daunst in greene meadowes, pincht maids in their sleep that swept not their houses cleane, and led poor Trauellers out of their way notoriously.'

II. i. 7. *moon's sphere.* According to the Ptolemaic system of astronomy accepted in Shakespeare's day, the sun, moon, and stars revolved about the earth fixed in transparent spheres.

II. i. 9. *orbs.* The circles of dark green grass often seen in old pastures, once supposed to be produced by the care of fairies in watering such spots.

II. i. 10. *pensioners.* Queen Elizabeth had a body-guard of tall and handsome gentlemen, many of them noble, who were called her pensioners.

II. i. 23. *changeling.* Fairies were supposed sometimes to steal a mortal child and to leave a substitute, usually of inferior intelligence, in its place. This substituted being was called a changeling; but here the word is used in reference to the stolen child.

II. i. 47. *gossip's bowl.* A drink, often called Lamb's-wool, made of ale, nutmeg, sugar, and roasted crab-apples. Originally served to the sponsors (gossips) at christenings, it was often used on other social occasions.

II. i. 54. *tailor.* This exclamation has called forth much learned discussion, the most amusing result of which has been Furness's suggestion that there is here a pun upon a word the reverse of 'header.'

II. i. 66. *Corin.* Corin and Phillida (Phyllis) were conventional names for a shepherd and shepherdess.

II. i. 78. *Perigenia.* 'This Sinnis had a goodly fair daughter called Perigouna, which fled away when she saw her father slain. . . . But Theseus finding her, called her, and sware by his faith he would use her gently, and do her no hurt, nor displeasure at all.' (North's *Plutarch*, ed. Skeat, p. 279.)

II. i. 79, 80. *Ægle . . . Antiopa.* 'For some say that Ariadne hung herself for sorrow, when she saw that Theseus had cast her off. Other . . . think that Theseus left her, because he was in love with another, as by these verses should appear: Ægles, the nymph, was loved of Theseus, Who was the daughter of Panopeus. . . . Philochorus, and some other hold opinion, that [Theseus] went thither with Hercules against the Amazons: and that to honour his valiantness, Hercules gave him Antiopa the Amazon. . . . Bion . . . saith, that he brought her away by deceit and stealth . . . and that Theseus enticed her to come into his ship . . . and so soon as she was aboard, he hoised his sail, and so carried her away.' (North's *Plutarch*, ed. Skeat, pp. 284-286.)

II. i. 98. *nine men's morris.* A game played upon a sort of chessboard dug in the turf.

II. i. 101-103. No interpretation of this puzzling passage is entirely satisfactory. E. K. Chambers paraphrases it thus: 'The summer is so bad that men wish it were winter. Not only have we offended the winds, but we have neglected the hymns and carols due from us to the moon. Therefore she too is wrathful, and does her part to spoil the weather.' Furness, on the other hand, explains it as follows: 'Here in Warwickshire, says Titania, in effect (for of course she and Oberon are in the Forest of Arden, with never a thought of Athens; who ever heard of the nine mens morris on the slopes of Pentelicus?), "here the poor human mortals have no summer with its sports, and now they have had no winter with its hymns and carols." ' If the latter be the meaning, 'therefore' is to be understood as 'because of our quarrel.'

II. i. 148-169. There is general agreement that this passage contains some allegory; but as to the extent and interpretation of this there is great diversity of opinion. It is fairly certain that the 'fair vestal throned by the west' is Queen Elizabeth. The imagery of the whole passage was very likely suggested by the allegorical figures which appeared in the pageants and 'triumphs' of the day, and it is not impossible that there is specific reference to the 'Princely Pleasures' with which the Earl of Leicester entertained Queen Elizabeth at Kenilworth in 1575.

II. i. 231. The story here 'changed,' i.e., reversed, is that of Apollo's pursuit of the nymph Daphne, who was transformed into a laurel tree and thus escaped.

III. i. 64. *bush of thorns.* English peasants saw 'the man in the moon' as bearing a bundle of sticks on his back.

III. i. 122, 123. *you see an ass-head of your own.*

A popular retort which is flung out by Bottom with no consciousness of its special appropriateness.

III. i. 138. *plain-song.* Just what characterization of the cuckoo's song is intended is not clear. Perhaps the comparison is between the simple musical interval of the cuckoo's song and that which often occurs at the end of a phrase in the chanting of the psalms. The bird's cry of 'Cuckoo' gives rise in the following lines to one of the common Elizabethan jokes about cuckolds.

III. i. 169. *Moth.* The meaning of this name appears when it is given its Elizabethan pronunciation, 'mote,' i.e., a minute particle, as of dust in a sunbeam.

III. ii. 25. *our stamp.* Those who are puzzled by the unexpected 'our' instead of 'my,' or who fail to see the alarming effect of the stamping of so diminutive a being, may escape the difficulty by adopting the emendation (first suggested by Allen) *at one stamp,* i.e., 'in one rush.' But cf. IV. i. 91, 92.

III. ii. 97. *costs the fresh blood dear.* An allusion to the once popular belief that sighing lowers vitality.

III. ii. 129. 'If Lysander's present protestations are true, they destroy the truth of his former vows to Hermia, and the contest between these two truths, which in themselves are holy, must in the issue be devilish and end in the destruction of both.' (W. A. Wright.)

III. ii. 213, 214. There is some doubt as to the extent to which Shakespeare here pushes his allusion to heraldry, but the following note is satisfactory enough: 'Helen exemplifies her position by a simile,— "we had *two of the first,* i.e., *bodies,* like the double coats [of arms] in heraldry that belong to man and wife *as one person,* but which, like our *single heart,* have but *one crest.*"' (Douce.)

III. ii. 257. The punctuation adopted in the text is the result of an attempt to make sense out of the

reading of the First Quarto: *No, no; heele Seeme.* As
the speech stands Demetrius must be supposed to address Hermia, and then, breaking off, to taunt Lysander. There is almost certainly some corruption of
the text, and it might be better to read with the First
Folio: *No, no, Sir, seeme to breake loose.* Then the
No, no, Sir! would have the force of the modern col-
loquialism, 'No you don't!'

III. ii. 329. *hindering knot-grass.* The knot-
grass, a low, tough weed, hinders growth in gardens,
and was popularly supposed to be a means of stunt-
ing a child's growth.

III. ii. 389. *the morning's love.* It is not certain
whether this phrase refers to Cephalus, according to
classical mythology a mighty hunter and the lover of
Aurora, the dawn, or whether it is a figurative de-
scription of Aurora herself, or whether it means
simply the sun. It is clear, however, that Oberon is
contrasting his freedom to sport by day with the fate
of those spirits which are exiled from the sunshine.

IV. i. 89 S. d. *Music, still.* This stage direction
of the Folio is puzzling. Since Oberon later directs
the music to sound, this may be a direction to the
musicians to be ready, but not to play. Another
possibility is that the meaning is simply 'soft music.'

IV. i. 145. *Saint Valentine.* An allusion to the
old belief that the birds began to mate on St. Valentine's day. Cf. Chaucer, *The Parlement of Foules:*

'For this was on seynt Valentynys day,
  Whan every bryd comyth there to chese his make . . .'

IV. i. 197, 198. 'Helena, I think, means to say
that having found Demetrius unexpectedly, she con-
sidered her property in him as insecure as that which
a person has in a jewel that he has found by accident;
which he knows not whether he shall retain, and

which, therefore, may properly enough be called his own and not his own.' (Malone.)

IV. i. 226. *at her death.* Does Bottom here mean Thisbe's death? But he is speaking, not of *the* play, but of *a* play. And why 'more gracious' after Thisbe's death? Theobald was very likely right in reading 'after death.' Were Bottom to rise, after dying a heroic death, and sing his 'ballad,' that would be gracious indeed.

V. i. 19, 20. 'The mere idea of a joy is enough incentive to a strong imagination to conjure up and believe in the actual presence of a something which causes that joy.' (Chambers.)

V. i. 79, 80. *intents . . . conn'd.* 'Intents' is here used in a double sense. Philostrate speaks of the clowns' endeavors to please as carried to the limit of their ability and of their having learned the play, the result of their endeavor, with painful toil.

V. i. 128 S. d. *Tawyer.* This reference in the stage direction of the First Folio to one of the actors in the company to which Shakespeare belonged is an interesting evidence that the Folio was printed from a stage-copy.

V. i. 200. *Limander.* Limander and Helen are blunders for Leander and Hero, just as Shafalus and Procrus are the closest the clowns can come to Cephalus and Procris. The two pairs of lovers thus referred to were typical instances of devotion.

V. i. 210. *Now is the mural down.* In place of this the First Quarto, which is the most reliable authority for the text of this play, has, *Now is the moon used.* That this latter version is almost certainly corrupt is shown, however, not only by the difficulty of finding in it a satisfactory meaning, but also by the fact that the First Folio substitutes, *Now is the morall downe.* Although the reading of the Folio can be interpreted as a pun on the senses 'moral obstacle' and 'wall all' (i.e., mure all), it still seems unlikely to be what Shakespeare wrote. In despair most editors have taken refuge in the emendation of Pope here adopted, despite the fact that it is open to serious objection both on literary grounds and because the noun 'mural' does not elsewhere appear as part of Shakespeare's vocabulary. The true reading seems irretrievably lost.

V. i. 246. *horns.* Moon's lantern had sides of horn instead of glass, so that there is a double significance in his reference to the horned, i.e., crescent, moon. Thereupon Demetrius makes the inevitable Elizabethan joke about the horns which were supposed to grow upon the head of the married man whose wife was unfaithful to him.

V. i. 314. *No . . . ace.* Demetrius attempts to make a pun on a second sense of 'die,' i.e., one of a pair of dice. Some editors have attempted to help out Demetrius' wit by taking the word as related to 'duo,' i.e., two. The Elizabethan pronunciation of 'ace' gives Theseus a chance for another pun.

V. i. 393. Hecate is called triple because she was as Luna a heavenly goddess, as Diana an earthly one, and as Hecate one of the lower world. When, as the moon-goddess, she disappears at the coming of the sun, the fairies accompany her car.

V. i. 428, 429. It is not improbable that these lines were printed in the wrong order and should be transposed.

APPENDIX A

Sources of the Play

For *A Midsummer Night's Dream,* as for one other early play, *Love's Labour's Lost,* and another very late one, *The Tempest,* Shakespeare seems to have devised a plot with relative independence. At any rate, nothing has been found which may properly be called the 'source' of *A Midsummer Night's Dream.* The most that can be said is that there are resemblances of detail between this play and some earlier narratives.

None of these, however, are of any great importance. It is possible, for example, that in writing about Theseus and Hippolyta, Shakespeare had in mind Chaucer's *Knight's Tale;* for there too this 'Duke of Athens' and his bride 'do observance to a morn of May,' and there the name of Philostrate appears. Shakespeare knew also North's translation of Plutarch's *Lives,* which contains a 'Life of Theseus,' and he very probably borrowed some details from this. He could have read the story of Pyramus and Thisbe in several versions, such as that in Chaucer's *Legend of Good Women,* in Ovid's *Metamorphoses,* or in Golding's translation of Ovid (1565). It is barely possible that he derived the suggestion for Oberon's magic 'love-juice' from the Spanish *Diana Enamorada* by Jorge de Montemayor; but if he read an English translation, it must have been in manuscript, for none was published until 1598. He could have found accounts of Robin Goodfellow in several books, and he seems to have met the name Titania in Ovid, where it is applied to Diana; yet his conception of the fairies and of Bottom and the other 'hempen homespuns' is not derived from books, but from the traditions of the countryside, from his own observation of simple men, and from his own imagination.

APPENDIX B

THE HISTORY OF THE PLAY

A Midsummer Night's Dream was first printed, in quarto, in 1600. A second quarto bears the same date on the title-page, but this was actually printed about 1619. The existence of the play some years before 1600 is proved by the fact that it is mentioned by Francis Meres in his *Palladis Tamia,* which was published in 1598. Those who seek to determine the date of composition more definitely than this are obliged to base their opinions upon internal evidence. Some critics see in Titania's speech about the confusion of the seasons (II. i. 88-114) a reference to the unusually cold, wet summer of 1594. Others, believing that the play was written to honor some great wedding, have attempted, without conspicuous success, to determine whose that wedding was. The result of these and other conjectures and of inferences drawn from the manner in which Shakespeare here handled his verse is that there is general agreement that the play was written not earlier than 1593 and not later than 1595.

In its original and complete form the play has been, until relatively recent years, among the less popular of Shakespeare's works, although in 1631 the Bishop of Lincoln got into trouble with the Puritans by allowing it to be performed—in whole or in part—at his house on a Sunday. An abridgment of the play with the title *The Merry Conceited Humours of Bottom the Weaver* was apparently acted in private during the period when the theaters were closed (1642-1660). Whether the performance which Pepys saw in 1662 and thought 'the most insipid ridiculous play that ever I saw in my life' was a representation of the play as Shakespeare wrote it is not certain, but in 1692 at any rate the original was displaced by an operatic version with music by Purcell, and from then until well on in the nineteenth century the records show only such perversions and adaptations as that produced by David Garrick in 1755, in which some very stupid songs replaced much of Shakespeare's text and in which the parts of Lysander and Hermia were given to Italian singers.

The credit for the restoration to the stage of something like the original play must be given to Tieck, a German translator of Shakespeare, who produced it at Berlin in 1827 with the incidental music by Mendelssohn which has since become famous. Some of the best performances of recent years have been given in Germany, notably the production by Max Reinhardt, which combined remarkable excellences with lapses of taste characteristically German.

In England and America productions reasonably faithful to the original text have been both frequent and popular since the performance by Mme. Vestris in 1840 at Covent Garden in London. The spectacular possibilities of the play and the popularity of Mendelssohn's music have so appealed to managers that the text has often been swamped in scenery and sound, but there must have been good acting in Augustin Daly's production (1888), when Theseus was played by Joseph Holland, Demetrius by John Drew, Lysander by Otis Skinner, and Helena by Ada Rehan. In 1903 the New Amsterdam Theater in New York was opened with a performance of the play characterized rather by lavish expenditure of money than by intelligence of acting or direction; at another revival in 1906, Miss Annie Russell attempted to play the part of Puck; and in 1915 Granville Barker offered to New York his London production, one which certainly displayed intelligence although its gilded fairies and its substitution of supposedly suggestive 'decorations' in place of realistic scenery aroused much hostile criticism.

APPENDIX C

THE TEXT OF THE PRESENT EDITION

The text of the present volume is, by permission of the Oxford University Press, that of the *Oxford Shakespeare,* edited by the late W. J. Craig, except for the following deviations:

1. The stage directions are those of the First Folio or the First Quarto, any alterations or additions being enclosed in square brackets. The indication of a second scene in the fifth act has been omitted and the lines renumbered accordingly.

2. A few minor changes in punctuation and in spelling (such as almanac for almanack, gawd for gaud, laugh for loff, and antic for antique) have been made. The spelling lanthorn has been retained only in the speeches of Moon, where it adds clearness to a jest.

3. The following alterations, all reversions to the readings of the First Quarto (save where otherwise indicated), have been made in the text, the reading of the Quarto and the present text preceding the colon, and that of Craig following it:

I. i. 69	Whether: Whe'r	
	191	I'll: I'd
	ii. 87	an (Q. and): as
II. i. 7	moon's: moone's	
	69	steep (F1): steppe
	78	Perigenia: Perigouna
	91	Hath: Have
	249	where: whereon
	ii. 2	third part: third (misprint ?)
III. i. 87	of: have	
	160	whether: whe'r
	ii. 48	the: knee
	81	whether: whe'r
	97	costs: cost

	144	This: That (misprint ?)
	171	to: with
	190	bare: bear
	199	sisters' vows (Q. sisters vowes): sister-vows
	201	is all: is it all
	204	needles: needls
	264	potion: poison
IV.i.	21	courtesy (F1): curtsy
	86	Silence a while: Silence, awhile
	172	as: as doth
	179	a: in
V.i.	281	beams: streams

APPENDIX D

SUGGESTIONS FOR COLLATERAL READING

Geoffrey Chaucer, *The Knight's Tale.*

W. W. Skeat, *Shakespeare's Plutarch* (1875). The Life of Theseus.

Frank Sidgwick, *Sources and Analogues of 'A Mid-summer-Night's Dream'* (1908). This contains the story of Pyramus and Thisbe as told by Ovid and much Elizabethan material about Robin Goodfellow.

H. H. Furness, *New Variorum Shakespeare: A Midsummer Night's Dream* (1895).

C. C. Clarke, *Shakespeare Characters* (1863).

D. J. Snider, *The Shakespearian Drama* (1887). *Midsummer Night's Dream.*

G. C. D. Odell, *'A Midsummer Night's Dream' on the New York Stage,* in *Shaksperian Studies,* ed. Matthews and Thorndike, Columbia University Press (1916).

INDEX OF WORDS GLOSSED

(Figures in full-faced type refer to page-numbers)

abate: **52** (III. ii. 432)
abridgment: **65** (V. i. 39)
aby: **42** (III. ii. 175)
Acheron: **49** (III. ii. 357)
act: **53** (III. ii. 464 S. d.)
adamant: **21** (II. i. 195)
address'd: **67** (V. i. 106)
admirable: **64** (V. i. 27)
Ægle: **17** (II. i. 79)
after-supper: **65** (V. i. 34)
against: **5** (I. i. 125); **40** (III. ii. 99)
alone: **41** (III. ii. 119)
amiable: **53** (IV. i. 2)
an: **11** (I. ii. 54)
an 'twere: **12** (I. ii. 87)
anon: **14** (II. i. 17)
antic: **63** (V. i. 3)
Antiopa: **17** (II. i. 80)
apprehend: **63** (V. i. 5)
approve: **26** (II. ii. 68)
argument: **45** (III. ii. 242)
artificial: **43** (III. ii. 203)

barm: **15** (II. i. 38)
barren: **37** (III. ii. 13)
bated: **7** (I. i. 190)
bay'd: **57** (IV. i. 119)
bells: **58** (IV. i. 129)
Bergomask dance: **76** (V. i. 361)
beshrew: **25** (II. ii. 54)
beteem: **5** (I. i. 131)
bill: **13** (I. ii. 109)
blows: **22** (II. i. 249)
bootless: **15** (II. i. 37)
bottle: **55** (IV. i. 38)
brakes: **22** (II. i. 227)
bully: **29** (III. i. 8)
buskin'd: **16** (II. i. 71)

canker-blossom: **46** (III. ii. 282)
capacity: **67** (V. i. 105)
Carthage queen: **7** (I. i. 173)
cat: **24** (II. ii. 30)
Cavalery: **54** (IV. i. 25)
changeling: **14** (II. i. 23)
cheer: **40** (III. ii. 96)
chide: **19** (II. i. 145)
chiding: **58** (IV. i. 121)
childing: **18** (II. i. 112)
choughs: **37** (III. ii. 21)
clerks: **67** (V. i. 93)
close: **37** (III. ii. 7)
clowns: **29** (III. i. S. d.)
coil: **48** (III. ii. 339)
collied: **6** (I. i. 145)
compact: **64** (V. i. 8)
con: **13** (I. ii. 104)
conceits: **2** (I. i. 33)
concern: **3** (I. i. 60)
confusion: **6** (I. i. 149)
consecrate: **78** (V. i. 424)
constancy: **64** (V. i. 26)
contagious: **17** (II. i. 90)
continents: **17** (II. i. 92)
Corin: **16** (II. i. 66)
counsel: **8** (I. i. 216)
courtesy: **54** (IV. i. 21)
coy: **53** (IV. i. 2)
crab: **15** (II. i. 48)
crazed: **4** (I. i. 92)
create: **78** (V. i. 414)
critical: **65** (V. i. 54)
cry mercy: **35** (III. i. 186)
curst: **47** (III. ii. 300)

darkling: **26** (II. ii. 86)
dear: **9** (I. i. 249)
device: **65** (V. i. 50)

discharge: **13** (I. ii. 96)
disfigure: **3** (I. i. 51)
dispatch: **57** (IV. i. 114)
distemperature: **18** (II. i. 106)
distill'd: **3** (I. i. 76)
dowager: **1** (I. i. 5)
drawn: **50** (III. ii. 402)

eglantine: **23** (II. i. 252)
Egypt: **64** (V. i. 11)
eight and six: **30** (III. i. 25)
eke: **32** (III. i. 100)
enforced: **36** (III. i. 209)
Ercles: **11** (I. ii. 31)
estate unto: **4** (I. i. 98)
ever: **6** (I. i. 150)
extort: **42** (III. ii. 160)
eyne: **9** (I. i. 242)

faint: **8** (I. i. 215)
fair: **7** (I. i. 182)
fall (let fall): **69** (V. i. 144)
fall (happen): **70** (V. i. 189)
fancy's: **6** (I. i. 155)
fantasy: **2** (I. i. 32)
favour: **7** (I. i. 186)
favours: **14** (II. i. 12); **55** (IV. i. 55)
feigning: **2** (I. i. 31)
fell: **14** (II. i. 20)
fierce: **56** (IV. i. 75)
fire: **33** (III. i. 115)
flew'd: **58** (IV. i. 126)
flourish: **67** (V. i. 107 S. d.)
fond: **27** (II. ii. 88)
for: **72** (V. i. 255)
for that: **21** (II. i. 220)
force: **38** (III. ii. 40)
fordone: **77** (V. i. 383)
forgeries: **17** (II. i. 81)
fountain: **17** (II. i. 84)
French-crown colour: **13** (I. ii. 98)
frolic: **77** (V. i. 396)

game: **9** (I. i. 240)
gawds: **2** (I. i. 33)
glance: **16** (II. i. 75)
gleek: **34** (III. i. 154)
gossip's bowl: **15** (II. i. 47)
grace: **27** (II. ii. 89)
gracious: **61** (IV. i. 226)
griffin: **22** (II. i. 232)

hands: **79** (V. i. 447)
haunted: **37** (III. ii. 5)
hearts: **62** (IV. ii. 27)
Helen: **64** (V. i. 11)
hempen   home-spuns: **32** (III. i. 82)
henchman: **18** (II. i. 121)
Hiems': **18** (II. i. 109)
hight: **69** (V. i. 141)
his: **49** (III. ii. 368)
hold up: **45** (III. ii. 239)
horns: **72** (V. i. 246)

imbrue: **76** (V. i. 352)
immediately: **2** (I. i. 45)
impeach: **21** (II. i. 214)
increase: **18** (II. i. 114)
injurious: **43** (III. ii. 195)
injury: **19** (II. i. 147)
intelligence: **9** (I. i. 248)
intend: **48** (III. ii. 333)

jealousy: **59** (IV. i. 150)
jole: **48** (III. ii. 338)
juvenal: **32** (III. i. 100)

kind: **3** (I. i. 54)
knacks: **2** (I. i. 34)
knot-grass: **48** (III. ii. 329)

lakin: **30** (III. i. 14)
latch'd: **38** (III. ii. 36)
leave: **54** (IV. i. 21)
leviathan: **20** (II. i. 174)
Limander: **71** (V. i. 200)
lingers: **1** (I. i. 4)
lion-fell: **72** (V. i. 229)
lob: **14** (II. i. 16)

lode-stars: **7** (I. i. 183)
long: **48** (III. ii. 339)
love-in-idleness: **20** (II. i. 168)
lovely: **44** (III. ii. 211)

making: **15** (II. i. 32)
manet: **5** (I. i. 127)
margent: **17** (II. i. 85)
marry: **10** (I. ii. 11)
mazed: **18** (II. i. 113)
mechanicals: **37** (III. ii. 9)
mew'd: **3** (I. i. 71)
minimus: **48** (III. ii. 329)
misgraffed: **6** (I. i. 137)
mispris'd: **39** (III. ii. 74)
misprision: **40** (III. ii. 90)
momentany: **6** (I. i. 143)
mood: **39** (III. ii. 74)
Moth: **35** (III. i. 169)
moused: **73** (V. i. 276)
mouth: **58** (IV. i. 129)
mural: **71** (V. i. 210)
murrion: **17** (II. i. 97)

naught: **62** (IV. ii. 15)
neaf: **54** (IV. i. 20)
nearly: **5** (I. i. 126)
neeze: **16** (II. i. 56)
night-rule: **37** (III. ii. 5)
nine men's morris: **17** (II. i. 98)
nowl: **37** (III. ii. 17)

observation: **57** (IV. i. 110)
o'ercharg'd: **66** (V. i. 85)
oes: **43** (III. ii. 188)
of: **29** (II. ii. 154)
offices: **23** (II. ii. 8)
or: **20** (II. i. 171)
orbs: **14** (II. i. 9)
orient: **55** (IV. i. 60)
other: **56** (IV. i. 72)
ounce: **24** (II. ii. 30)
ousel-cock: **34** (III. i. 131)
overwatch'd: **77** (V. i. 375)
owe: **26** (II. ii. 79)

pale: **14** (II. i. 4)
palpable-gross: **77** (V. i. 376)
pard: **24** (II. ii. 31)
parlous: **30** (III. i. 14)
parted: **60** (IV. i. 195)
passing: **14** (II. i. 20)
passion: **74** (V. i. 295)
patched: **61** (IV. i. 216)
patches: **37** (III. ii. 9)
patent: **4** (I. i. 80)
paved: **17** (II. i. 84)
Peascod: **36** (III. i. 195)
pelting: **17** (II. i. 91)
pensioners: **14** (II. i. 10)
Perigenia: **17** (II. i. 78)
personage: **47** (III. ii. 292)
pert: **1** (I. i. 13)
Phibbus: **11** (I. ii. 38)
Philomel: **24** (II. ii. 13)
Phœbe: **8** (I. i. 209)
pilgrimage: **3** (I. i. 75)
plain-song: **34** (III. i. 138)
point: **28** (II. ii. 119)
points: **68** (V. i. 118)
pomp: **1** (I. i. 15)
possess'd: **4** (I. i. 100)
preferred: **63** (IV. ii. 40)
prey: **29** (II. ii. 150)
proper: **12** (I. ii. 89)
protest: **4** (I. i. 89)
purple-in-grain: **13** (I. ii. 98)

quail: **74** (V. i. 294)
quaint: **23** (II. ii. 7)
quell: **74** (V. i. 294)
quern: **15** (II. i. 36)
questions: **22** (II. i. 235)
quill: **34** (III. i. 134)
quire: **16** (II. i. 55)

recorder: **68** (V. i. 124)
rent: **44** (III. ii. 215)
repair: **56** (IV. i. 73)
rere-mice: **23** (II. ii. 4)
respect: **21** (II. i. 224)

respects: **6** (I. i. 160)
rheumatic diseases: **17** (II. i. 105)
right: **47** (III. ii. 302)
ringlets: **17** (II. i. 86)
roundel: **23** (II. ii. 1)
russet-pated: **37** (III. ii. 21)

sad: **45** (III. ii. 237)
saddest: **15** (II. i. 51)
sanded: **58** (IV. i. 126)
scrip: **10** (I. ii. 3)
self-affairs: **5** (I. i. 113)
sensible: **70** (V. i. 184)
sheen: **15** (II. i. 29)
shrewd: **15** (II. i. 33)
since: **19** (II. i. 149)
sinister: **69** (V. i. 165)
Sisters Three: **76** (V. i. 344)
snuff: **72** (V. i. 256)
soft: **58** (IV. i. 133)
something: **47** (III. ii. 304)
sort (n.): **37** (III. ii. 13)
sort (vb.): **49** (III. ii. 352)
sorting: **65** (V. i. 55)
sphery: **27** (II. ii. 99)
spite: **43** (III. ii. 194)
spleen: **6** (I. i. 146)
spring: **17** (II. i. 82)
square: **15** (II. i. 30)
Squash: **36** (III. i. 195)
stay: **22** (II. i. 235); **73** (V. i. 261)
steep: **16** (II. i. 69)
still: **8** (I. i. 212)
stop: **68** (V. i. 120)
streak: **23** (II. i. 257)
swound: **29** (II. ii. 154)

tailor: **16** (II. i. 54)
tall: **69** (V. i. 146)
Taurus': **41** (III. ii. 141)
tear: **11** (I. ii. 32)
tender: **39** (III. ii. 87)
that: **15** (II. i. 30)
Thisne: **11** (I. ii. 56)

Thracian singer: **65** (V. i. 49)
thorough: **14** (II. i. 3)
thread: **74** (V. i. 293)
thrum: **74** (V. i. 293)
'tide: **71** (V. i. 207)
tiring-house: **29** (III. i. 5)
tongs: **54** (IV. i. 33)
touch: **39** (III. ii. 70)
toward: **32** (III. i. 84)
toys: **63** (V. i. 3)
trace: **15** (II. i. 25)
translated: **7** (I. i. 191)
transported: **62** (IV. ii. 4)
trim: **42** (III. ii. 157)
triple Hecate: **77** (V. i. 393)
triumph: **1** (I. i. 19)
triumphantly: **57** (IV. i. 95)
troth: **25** (II. ii. 36)
Troyan: **7** (I. i. 174)
tuneable: **7** (I. i. 184)

unbreath'd: **66** (V. i. 74)
uncouple: **57** (IV. i. 113)

vaward: **57** (IV. i. 111)
versing: **16** (II. i. 67)
virtuous: **49** (III. ii. 367)
votaress: **18** (II. i. 123)

wanton: **17** (II. i. 99)
warrant: **75** (V. i. 328)
waxen: **16** (II. i. 56)
weed: **23** (II. i. 256)
which: **75** (V. i. 326)
wind: **57** (IV. i. 108 S. d.)
with: **38** (III. ii. 55)
withering out: **1** (I. i. 6)
without: **59** (IV. i. 159)
witnesseth: **64** (V. i. 25)
wood: **20** (II. i. 192)
worm: **39** (III. ii. 71)
wrath: **14** (II. i. 20)
wrong: **49** (III. ii. 361)

FANTASY + ILLUSION DIFFICULT TO
SEPARATE FROM REALITY — WHICH IS REAL?
DREAM VS. REALITY RECURRENT THEME FOR
SHAKESPEARE. WORLD OF ILLUSION + DREAM IS
PART OF REALITY. DREAMS ARE SHADOWS OF
REALITY. SEE ACT IV ii. P. 60-61